GARLAND STUDIES ON

INDUSTRIAL PRODUCTIVITY

edited by
STUART BRUCHEY
ALLAN NEVINS PROFESSOR EMERITUS
COLUMBIA UNIVERSITY

A GARLAND SERIES

DOWNSIZING ISSUES

THE IMPACT ON EMPLOYEE MORALE AND PRODUCTIVITY

Bonita J. Manson

GARLAND PUBLISHING, INC.
A MEMBER OF THE TAYLOR & FRANCIS GROUP
NEW YORK & LONDON/2000

Published in 2000 by
Garland Publishing, Inc.
A member of the Taylor & Francis Group
29 West 35th Street
New York, NY 10001

10 9 8 7 6 5 4 3 2 1

Library of Congress Cataloging-in-Publication Data

Manson, Bonita J.
   Downsizing issues : the impact on employee morale and productivity / Bonita J. Manson.
      p. cm. — (Garland studies on industrial productivity)
   Originally presented as the author's thesis (doctoral—Kansas State University).
   Includes bibliographical references and index.
   ISBN 0-8153-3525-3 (alk. paper)
   1. County officials and employees—United States—Case studies. 2. County government—United States—Personnel management—Case studies. 3. Downsizing of organizations—United States—Case studies. 4. Employee morale—United States—Case studies. 5. Government productivity—United States—Case studies. I. Title. II. Series.

JS411 .M36 1999
331.11'8—dc21
                                                      99-044622

Printed on acid-free, 250 year-life paper
Manufactured in the United States of America

Contents

List of Tables

Acknowledgments

I wish to again thank my major professor, James B. Boyer retired and the Dean of the College of Education, Michael Holen at Kansas State University for their assistance and support throughout my studies. A special thanks to my doctoral supervisory committee, John Hortin, Mary E. Griffith, Stephen Bollman, and Carol Oukrop, chairperson for their critique of my dissertation from which this text is formed. In particular, I would like to extend my appreciation and thanks to the University Cooperative Extension Service in California and Illinois for their willingness to support research on implication for leadership training in face of downsizing.

Again, I am indebted to my esteemed former professors and colleagues for their support and guidance F. Afana, R. Bonnila, E. Chism, B. Bergman, C. Garrett, A. Green, E. Soccio (deceased), J. Spears, and F. Web, E.T., Williamson. Finally, I deeply appreciate the moral support of my family and friends, especially to my husband Tony J. Manson and sons, Tony, Jr. and Gregory.

CHAPTER I

Introduction

Today's economy, advances in technology, and increased competition for dollars have caused many organizations to reevaluate their goals and prospects for survival. The focus is on restructuring, reorganizing, and re-engineering their organizations (Caudron, 1996). Many companies are undergoing budget cuts, becoming more cost-conscious and trying to do more with less. The trend for businesses has been to cut labor cost to trim expenses (Winston James and Li-Ping Tang, 1996).

Gottlieb and Conkling (1995) reported that downsizing escalated in 1992. In fact, some companies experienced a more significant organizational change.

March 1992 - Reporting a loss of 4.5 billion for the year, GM announced the closing of twelve plants - representing 16,000 jobs - a down payment on a previously announced plan to fire 74,000 workers by 1995.

July 1992 - In a major setback for its subsidiary, Hughes Aircraft Company, General Motors Corporation (GM) as a result of its move into the defense business took a $749.4 million write-off in the second quarter. This was expected to result in 9,000 more layoffs.

Amoco, Unocal, and Mobil announced major business restructurings. Amoco said it cut 85,000 jobs. Unocal planned to eliminate 1,100 of its 17,000 jobs worldwide, mostly in the United

States. Mobil said it would cut 2,000 salaried jobs or 9.5 percent
of that group.

August 1992 - Manufacturing employment continued to drop
to 97,000 jobs in August, capping three years of almost steady
decline.

September 1992 - International Business Machines Corporation
(IBM) announced that a total of 40,000 jobs would be eliminated
this year through buyouts (Gottlieb & Conkling, 1995).

The following year, 1993, there was a record set for the number of jobs cut. The first ten months of 1994, announced job cuts
slowed down to 460,063 reported Gottlieb and Conkling (1995).
However, by the end of 1994, Auster (1995) stated, nearly 600,000
jobs were eliminated in U.S. companies due to global competition
and economic recession.

Cuts were also experienced by the public sector and even the
military. During the third quarter of 1991, employment dropped
by 84,000 jobs at the state and local government level (Winston
James & Li-Ping Tang, 1996). In the United States, the number of
military personnel was reduced more than 30 percent after the pas-
sage of a public law accounting for job loss of over a million people (Cameron, 1994). Like other organizations, as reported by the
Strategic Planning Council (1991), "Cooperative Extension faces an
era of discontinuous futures."

> Rebirth, renewal, and right sizing describe organizational changes
> occurring in the Cooperative Extension System. 'No state is
> exempt from restructuring. Life in the future will be very dif-
> ferent from the past - more difficult to predict yet requiring
> greater and faster adaptation. Organizations will face an end to
> the business they've perceived themselves to be in and a need
> to redirect human and financial resources. The challenge is to
> chart a course compatible with the changing environment and
> drop programs and activities that deal with obsolete situations
> (Harriman and Daugherty, 1992).

Technology, the global economy, funding sources, and a shift
in population will greatly impact Extension operations in the

twenty-first century. Delivery and dissemination of information will be different. Clientele needs will change because the population will have shifted from rural, family farms, and young to urban, commercial farms, and older. There is also a growing minority population. Harriman and Daugherty (1992) stated, "Extension must be seen as an organization staffed to meet the needs of a broader, more diverse population."

Previously, reductions in the work force were generally a short-term temporary occurrence until the economy improved. However, the reductions are now becoming permanent. When the cuts are a one time occurrence implemented for a more efficient operation, the employees who survive are relieved. However, after successive work force reductions, some survivors are unable to cope with the trauma of these reductions.

Even though restructuring leads to clearer directions, Harriman and Daugherty (1992) stated, "It has often meant chaos, stress, resistance, and conflict for Extension professionals." When downsizing is done for fiscal reasons, employees may perceive the organization as untrustworthy, resulting in a lower level of personal commitment to the job, stated Ewing (1994). Overall, downsizing can have a negative impact on the employees who remain with the organization. Job security vanishes in the organizations' effort to become leaner and more efficient. Those who believed they would have their jobs for life no longer have job security. Their insecurities reduced their confidences in the organization's leadership and direction (Lehrer, 1997). Some of these employees may subsequently experience low morale and feelings of helplessness. Anger, resentment, guilt, anxiety, withdrawal, and apathy may also result because of their uncertainty of how they will fit into the new leaner organization (Brockner, Davy, & Carter, 1985; Ting, 1996; Winston James & Li-Ping Tang, 1996; and Lehrer, 1997).

ALTERNATIVES TO LAYOFFS

President Gardner reported that the University of California's operating budget, supported by the States' general fund, fell short $163 million of the Regents' requested amount in 1990–91 (ANR Report, 1990). This shortfall had a great impact on the Division of Agriculture and Natural Resources (DANR) programs, stated President Gardner (primarily a 5 percent legislatively mandated

reduction in state funded research, public service, and administration). "For DANR, these reductions totaled $4.2 million for
(Agriculture Experiment Station) AES (50 percent of the University's state-funded organized research) and $2.1 million for (Coop-
erative Extension) CE (80 percent of the University's state-funded
public service)," stated Vice-president Farrell, 1991.

Vice-president Farrell advised the Divisions' Program Managers
to revise their budgets to reflect the 5 percent reductions. He stated:

> In adjusting to the 1990–91 reductions, we will seek to maintain
> the viability of our highest priority research and extension
> programs. Not all programs will be affected uniformly by the
> reduction. Wherever possible we must look to consolidation of
> programs and functions, reduction of administrative costs, elim-
> ination of redundant services and inefficiencies (ANR Report,
> September 1990).

A voluntary early retirement incentive plan (VERIP) for both
faculty and staff was also presented to the Regents, President
Gardner announced (ANR Report, September, 1990).

Along with state funding, the University of California also
received about 20 percent from the federal government and nearly
17 percent from the counties that same year. The federal funds
were a substantial increase, stated Farrell. However, they did not
offset the reduction in the state-funded budget (Farrell, 1991).
Additionally, the fiscal conditions of many California counties
were extremely tight and tenuous, he stated (Farrell, 1991).

The following actions were taken by Cooperative Extension,
after extensive review of program priorities, existing budget and
personnel commitments, and options for meeting the mandated
budget reductions:

1. Elimination of temporary salary savings of $398,000 which
    includes the projected 1990–91 VERIP (academic and non-
    academic) savings of $165,000;
2. Elimination of 4.0 CE vacancies and 2.7 CE non-academic
    vacancies in the regions and campuses for a reduction of
    $218,000;
3. Elimination of $193,000 in funding for CE non-salary oper-
    ating expenses at campuses and regions;

4. Elimination of $200,000 in funding for CE special programs and projects;
5. Elimination of $246,000 in funding of CE academic support units;
6. Elimination of $139,000 in funding of administrative services (6.3 percent); and
7. Elimination of $362,000 in benefits provisions attributed to elimination of vacant positions and in other provisions (Farrell, 1991).

The 1991–1992 reductions for AES of about $4 million and $1.7 million for CE were the second in succession for California's Extension programs. It was reported that the budget shortfalls were the University of California's worst budget in more than 20 years (ANR Report, July 25, 1991). The state budget resulted in another 5 percent reduction for Cooperative Extension which in turn resulted in the Regents freezing merit increases for all University employees for the 1991–92 fiscal year (ANR Report, July 25, 1991). The additional $17.5 million cut to University funds was $312.5 million less than what was needed to maintain CE's current programs (ANR Report, July 25, 1991). The Regents also approved two new voluntary programs to cut payroll costs. Employees could retire early or reduce their work hours. Under these plans:

The Voluntary Early Retirement Incentive Program (VERIP) called 'Take 5,' was for eligible UC Retirement Plan (UCRP) members only. Employees under the Public Employees Retirement System (PERS) were not given the option.

'Take 5' had a lower criterion for years of service/age. It added an extra five years of service credit in the calculation used to determine the employee's retirement income. It also offered a transition payment of about three months' salary.

The Time Reduction Incentive Plan (TRIP-92) gave most UC employees the option of scaling back their work hours from 10 percent to 25 percent for a 12 months or 18 months period with management approval. TRIP-92 allowed any Division employee, not represented by a bargaining agreement like unions, to reduce their hours for a designated period. Employees who elected to participate in TRIP-92 had to complete the contract as specified.

Since the program was available to both full and part-time employees, staff had to work at least 20 hours per week to maintain their existing health benefits. Employees on TRIP-92 were subject to the same layoff policies as other UC employees, but not to across-the-board salary reductions. Employees received bonus leave (the vacation hours lost in the reduction) plus extra hours for taking part in the program (ANR Report, July 23, 1992).

Cooperative Extension lost a total of 110 employees under UC's voluntary early retirement options in 1991 (ANR Report, July 23, 2992). The permanent work force reduced staff nearly 2,000 according to UC officials (ANR Report, July 23, 1992).

The budget is a $255 million reduction from the January budget proposed by the governor, and a reduction of $224 million from the level of funding received by the University in 1991–92.

To put it in perspective, this year's appropriation provides UC with the same amount of money it received in 1987, despite our growth in workload, increase in number of students and without adjusting for inflation (ANR Report, July 23, 1992).

According to Vice-president Farrell, the Division had to absorb a permanent 6 percent cut in 1992–93 and an approximate additional 4 percent permanent cut in 1993–94. He stated,

"I cannot overemphasize the seriousness of the situation. Coupled with two successive 5 percent cuts, UC's public service programs (primarily Cooperative Extension) and research will have been reduced by 20 percent in the last three years."

Farrell continued, "There is simply no way we can carry on business as usual. Nor can we take these cuts across the board without jeopardizing the quality of all our programs. Cuts will have to be made selectively. Some programs may have to be sacrificed to protect the excellence and integrity of our highest priority program" (ANR Report, July 23, 1992).

THE ISSUES

The psychological issues often are ignored by management during downsizing. Management efforts are concentrated on effectively implementing layoffs or alternatives to layoffs. Only a few organizations have slowly developed skills so that the work force reductions do not cause job security crisis (Tomasko, 1987). According to Levinson (1976), when the organizations do not account for the experience of loss, changes in the organization are unsuccessful. People are unable to cope when they have feelings of helplessness within their environment. The charge of management in downsized organizations is to create a culture that helps fill the vacuum left by the reorganization (Tomasko, 1987).

There is a need for organizations to reestablish a relationship of trust, loyalty, and commitment, if they want their downsized company to survive. Surviving employees need assurance that they are not being shafted. While many organizations offer attrition programs, such as early retirement to avoid layoffs, some employees feel they have no choice but to retire. They worry about being next in line for layoff. Their worries consequently lead to stress, which in turn might result in a decline in their job performance. According to Caudron (1996), the success of downsizing depends on whether the company:

1. Provides career management assistance;
2. Acknowledges survivors' emotional needs;
3. Communicates after the downsizing; and
4. Clarifies new roles.

Sugalski, Manzo, and Meadows (1995) stated, "By moving toward an employment strategy that understands the needs, values, and expectations of the existing and potential applicant population, it may help define and reestablish a psychological contract to which employees can commit." Other researchers agreed that when organizations understand the human reactions to change, they can better prepare for future reductions with the least amount of distress for their employees (Maynard, 1996; Nelton, 1996; Winston James & Li-Ping Tang, 1996; and Neal, 1996).

RESEARCHING THE ISSUES

The purpose of this study is threefold. The researcher attempted to find out how downsizing in Cooperative Extension affected job performance, employee morale, and trust (in the workplace). The Manson's Workplace Inventory Analysis is an original instrument

designed to secure reaction on downsizing from employees of
Cooperative Extension, specifically on Morale, Survivor Job Security, and Trust (in the workplace). Items 1–6 and 13 are related to
information which impacts how employees feel about their work
environment. Item 7–12 and 19 addressed Workplace Morale;
15–18 and 20 were devoted to Survivor Job Security; and 14 and
21–26 were related to Trust (in the workplace). The researcher was
concerned with issues of morale and productivity, while noting factors of advanced training and seniority in Cooperative Extension
employment. There has been particular attention to the difference
of perception between staff employees and those with managerial
or supervisory responsibilities.

Cooperative Extension Service is a nonformal educational
network which combines the expertise and resources of federal,
state, and local governments. The program priorities, organizational structures, and external relationships not only changes as
the needs change, but also as the funding changes. The research
was undertaken in hopes of providing recommendations for
leadership training.

SIGNIFICANCE OF THE STUDY

Most studies tended to focus on antecedents or consequences of
layoffs (Brockner, 1988). Not until more recently did researchers
start to concentrate more on the impact of layoffs for the surviving
work force (Blonder, 1976; Brockner, 1988; and Greenhalgh, 1982).
Brockner's (1988) partial listing of some of the potential psychological states survivors' experience include:

(a.) job insecurity, e.g., if employees perceive that additional
      downsizing is in the offering;
(b.) positive inequity, e.g., if employees perceive that they did not
      'deserve' to remain, relative to their dismissed co-workers;
(c.) anger, e.g., if survivors believe that the methods of the lay-
      off, or even the very existence of the layoffs were inappro-
      priate and
(d.) relief, e.g., if survivors were worried prior to the layoffs that
      they would be dismissed.

Furthermore, he stated, "The psychological states that layoffs
evoke have the potential to affect survivors' work behavior and

attitudes" (Brockner, 1988). These psychological states could lead to impaired performance, a significant boost in work motivation, or even greater tension among survivors (Brockner, 1988).

Reports on the empirical investigation of the multiple causes, consequences and dynamics of downsizing are limited (Cameron, 1994). Most downsizing efforts have been unsuccessful in the past. There are no set guidelines or principles for companies to follow. The only guide used by most companies is their own past downsizing experience, anecdotal data from colleagues who have downsized, or a gut feel for what is right (Cameron, 1994).

SIGNIFICANCE FOR EDUCATION

The significance of this study to education is to improve the administration in Extension Services faced with downsizing by providing a design for leadership training. When downsized and restructured organizations ignore human variables, productivity suffers and employees' morale and motivation decrease, according to Trahant and Burke (1996). If change is inevitable, organizations need to be able to effectively manage it.

The primary role of Extension is to plan pertinent programs that are effective in meeting the educational needs of the community in agriculture, family and consumer studies, and youth development. This study focuses on maintaining professional competence with less staff. The results of this study can be used in designing Educational Leadership training programs for community based organizations and others faced with downsizing.

RESEARCH OBJECTIVES

1. To determine whether the morale of employees can improve in a downsized organization.
2. To determine if the job performance of survivors can improve after downsizing.
3. To determine whether trust can be rebuilt after layoffs.

RESEARCH QUESTIONS

1. What impact does downsizing have on survivors?
2. How does management's perception of the impact of downsizing on productivity differ from employees' perception?

(Is there a difference in perception of downsizing on productivity between management and employees?)
3. Can employee morale improve, if management provides favorable incentive?

DEFINITION OF TERMS

Downsizing is the planned elimination of positions or jobs. It does not include the discharge of individual for cause, or individual departures via normal retirement or resignations (Cascio, 1993).

Employee Morale is the mental and emotional condition of staff in the work environment. It is the level of psychological well-being based on job.

Furlough is an unpaid leave of absence for a pre-specified time. The person's job is guaranteed at the period's end.

Impact is the way employees are affected by their job surroundings.

Layoffs is a permanent, involuntary separation of individuals from an organization due to a need to cut costs. It is the dismissals that are permanent rather than temporary, and not due to inappropriate or inadequate work behavior (Brockner, 1988).

Productivity is the rate at which goods or services are produced. It is the output per unit of labor.

Psychological contract is an emotional bond between employer and employee. It is implicit and thus unofficial and includes mutual responsibilities and expectations (Matbys and Burack, 1993).

Pull strategies are plans which generally involve offering, for a limited time, some inducement to all or a subgroup of employees encouraging them to resign voluntarily (Tomasko, 1987).

Redeployment is the reassignment of employees within an organization. The new assignment may or may not be equal to the previous position held.

Re-engineering is the process of structuring an organization for change.

Reorganizing is the process of undergoing a change. It involves making changes within an organization.

Restructuring is an arrangement of different parts of a complex entity. A term used to describe downsizing.

Severance pay is the continued payment of salary for a time after layoff (Ting, 1996).

Survivors are the persons who are left after an organization downsizes.

Transition assistance is the outplacement and retraining assistance provided to employees (Ting, 1996).

LIMITATIONS OF THE STUDY

The design of this study recognized certain limitations. These limitations are:

1. This study was limited to 58 county based staff working in Cooperative Extension offices in the states of California and Illinois.
2. The investigator had previous work experiences as a member of the professional staff in Cooperative Extension.
3. The results were valid to the extent that the respondents answered the questions honestly.
4. Participants had an opportunity to decline participation.
5. The two groups were not homogeneous. Therefore, no comparisons were made.
6. This study was limited to Cooperative Extension staff located in county offices affected by downsizing in the states of California and Illinois. The conclusions drawn from this study will be limited to generalization to similar institutions.

CHAPTER 2

Review of Related Literature

It is not unusual for organizations to experience some form of organizational change in today's competitive market. The trend of
doing more with less has corporate America slashing overhead any
way they can. Employees can no longer expect that in exchange for
loyal service, they will enjoy a lifetime of employment with benefits
(Burack & Singh, 1995). In the process of companies cutting cost,
Burack and Singh (1995) stated that millions of jobs are eliminated
with no end in sight. The list of companies announcing consecutive
waves of downsizing is growing daily according to Burack and
Singh (1995). What was once considered an unusual practice experienced by companies in trouble became the norm for many organizations undergoing a change (Cameron, 1994). Cascio (1993) stated
downsizing appeared to be endemic to the 1990s. Many well-known
companies (American Telephone & Telegraph, Eastman Kodak,
Citicorp, Goodyear, Digital Equipment, Amoco, Chevron, Exxon,
Black & Decker and others) have reported corporate restructuring
(Cascio, 1993). This norm has also moved into the federal government with the creation of the National Performance Review in 1993
(Lehrer, 1997).

Downsizing efforts have drastically changed during the 1990s.
The elimination of jobs is only not affecting blue collar workers, but
a disportionately high number of white collar workers. Cascio (1993)
stated, "while middle managers make up only five to eight percent
of the work force, they accounted for seventeen percent of all dismissals from 1989 to 1991. Further evidence comes from the fact
that in 1992 white-collar employees constituted thirty-six percent
during the 1982 slump."

Whetten (1988) discussed evidence of the pervasiveness of decline. He stated:

1. Decreased enrollments caused cut backs in schools.
2. Recessionary pressures resulted in record number of layoffs in industry.
3. The military scaled its operations.
4. Non-support at many churches forced churches to close their doors.
5. Declining revenues curtailed the municipal services (Whetten, 1988).

Decline affects society as a whole, especially when an entire industry retrenches. The family is affected by unemployment. The morale of the surviving employees deteriorated when the remaining employees were forced to deal with fewer resources stated Whetten (1988).

Most companies that reorganize, restructure, or downsize often fail to achieve positive results. While organizations were equipped to plan and implement change, they tend to be unaware of the human aspects of change. Demers et. al. (1996) stated employees can be very resistant to change because they want to hold on to what is familiar to them. Nobody wants to risk failure. As a result, the employees find themselves coping with stress rather than performing their duties. Eventually, the decreased productivity causes the employer to lean on staff, who in return becomes more anxious, resulting in a destructive cycle.

Declining resources impact an organization considerably. First, Whetten (1980) stated, the way employees think and their career patterns, as well as how the organization conducts business, are affected by retrenchment. Fewer resources lessens the margin for error. If a bad decision is made, it can be harmful to the survival of a declining firm. The increased tension and pressure may lead to lower morale and a higher turnover of employees (Behn, 1978 and Levine, 1979). Secondly, decline may increase interpersonal conflicts (Whetten, 1980). Third, Whetten (1980) felt that employees who can least afford it, or in some cases least deserve it, are the ones who are penalized at both the individual and organizational level. During downsizing, Levine (1978) stated, the low-skilled, low-income, minority, young, and very old staff members are the ones who have the most difficulty absorbing the loss of wages and finding new jobs. Finally, the rate of organizational innovation is affected, but how much is not agreed upon, stated Whetten (1980).

Borucki and Barnett (1990) stated only a few empirical studies have been conducted on organizational decline. Earlier studies referred to decline in two ways: "decline-as-cutbacks and decline-as-stagnation," stated Whetten (1980). Cameron et. al. (1988) stated, "Decline has more recently been defined as a two-stage phenomenon in which, first, an organization's ability to adapt to its domain, or micro-niche, deteriorates, and second, resources are reduced within the organization."

Tomasko (1987) discussed one of the recent approaches to managing decline called "demassing programs." Characteristically, a demassing program includes:

1. Relatively large reductions (5–15 percent and more of the middle-level work force);
2. Widespread cutbacks that affect the many, if not all, divisions and departments;
3. Deep reductions that usually cover several levels of the organization;
4. Priority on lowering costs by lowering head count; and
5. Emphasis on completing the program as quickly as possible (p. 29).

While some businesses viewed demassing as a way for the companies to survive, others saw it as a convenient rationale for postponing decreased earnings as a result of poor management stated, Borucki and Barnett (1990).

Corporations have been laying off personnel by the thousands over the past years to downsize their companies. Many dismissed employees felt they were being sacrificed, especially those who were in their fifties, stated Van Buren III (1996). Downsizing not only affects the employees, but the family and community as well. When corporations undergo restructuring, it is important that its programs, policies, and communication reflect an understanding and willingness to help ameliorate the damage caused by downsizing, stated Van Buren III (1996). Reece (1996) agreed that a formalized communication plan can and should play a key role in organizational change and the development of corporate cultures.

Communities are important to the success of businesses. Van Buren III (1996) said, "Unless corporations are willing to make the case that mass dismissals are necessary, and do so in language that is credible and believable, they should not be surprised when communities protest and populists attempt to gain advantage at their expense (p. 50)."

Rubach (1995) suggested that companies reexamine how they manage their business if they want to become competitive and increase their productivity. He stated some companies tried to improve their internal efficiency rather than react to economic recessions (Rubach, 1995). The downsizing efforts, for these companies, were focused on redesigned work processes that improved productivity rather than on last ditch survival efforts.

Researchers agreed that downsizing enables an organization to become more viable and competitive if good implementation is involved in the plan (Roach, 1996; Winston James & Li-Ping Tang, 1996; Armstrong-Stassen & Latack, 1992; and Borucki & Barnett, 1990). Rubach (1995) also stated organizational downsizing, during the past decade, was used as an initiative to increase the productivity of American firms. However, a poorly planned reduction in the the work force can have the opposite effect. Instead of organizations experiencing growth, the poorly implemented cutbacks can result in decreased productivity, burnout, low morale, and/or bizarre behaviors. Jane Capanizzi-Mook, President of JCM Enterprises, said, "Studies have shown that one-half of the companies that have downsized have the same or lower levels of productivity, and employees have low morale, distrust of management, and fear of future downsizing" (Rubach, 1995). If the wrong people, levels, or functions are removed during downsizing, the company is negatively impacted. "Some economists and industrial psychologists contend that downsizing can hurt companies more than help them," stated Bridges (1994). Therefore, companies need to be cautious about the way the layoffs are handled, if they want to function effectively after downsizing.

Stamps (1996) stated that in companies'quest to compete in the new global economy, they are no longer able to serve their clientele. They cut staff to become leaner and what they believe to be more efficient. But in reality, they are left with insufficient human resources to serve existing customers or to generate new customers and new revenue, stated Stamps (1996). He quoted, Peter Drucker,

"In many, if not most cases, downsizing has turn out to be something that surgeons for centuries have warned against: amputation before diagnosis. The result is always a casualty" (Stamps, 1996). In fact, Stamps (1996) said, "When work force reductions fail to deliver the desired boost to the bottom line, the next recourse has been to . . . well, cut some more." He quoted Dwight Gertz of Mercer Management Consulting in Boston "Companies have grown addicted to downsizing as a way to bolster the bottom line" (Stamps, 1996).

While downsizing is expected to yield both economic and organizational benefit, a 1991 survey by the Wyatt Company of 1,005 firms suggested that most restructuring efforts fall short of their established objectives:

- Only forty-six percent of the companies said their cuts reduced expenses enough over time, in part because four times out of five, managers ended-up replacing some of the very people they had dismissed;
- Fewer than one in three said profits increased as much as expected; and
- only twenty-one percent reported satisfactory improvements in shareholder's return on investment (p.98).

Layoffs are often used to cut labor cost due to unfavorable business conditions. Survivors of layoffs responded to work behaviors and attitudes, such as productivity and organizational commitment in very different ways (Brockner, 1988). Rubach (1995) believed the quality of an organization can survive if the company makes it clear that they value their employees. After downsizing, it is important that the company pays attention to their remaining employees. She stated, "Senior management needs to be honest and sincere about what has happened in the organization and provide employees with information about where the business is headed" (Rubach, 1995). Many of these employees are fearful about losing their jobs, have decreased loyalty to their organizations, and feel guilty about retaining their jobs when co-workers have lost theirs (Rubach, 1995).

Job security is no longer based on loyal service to the employer. Fox (1996) stated the employees must determine how their performance can benefit the organization, if they are going to survive. He cited his new relationship between employer and employees, as it was reported in Fortune magazine, June 13, 1994:

> There will never be job security. You will be employed by us as
> long as you add value to the organization, and you are continu-
> ously responsible for finding ways to add value (Fox, 1996).

Kuttner (1993) suggested that businesses cannot expect employees to be team players when there is a lack of job security or the
business is operated by management and contingent employees.
Temporary workers are less likely to be committed to the goals of
the organization. They do not have a vested interest in the organization. After all, their status is only temporary. These employees are
less likely to be committed to an organization that does not have an
investment in them. The employees who remain with the company
have an added burden of training other staff members and handling the added work load. This resulted in longer work hours, more
stress, and subsequently workers' burn out. The work environment
becomes less creative and productive because employees are unsure
of what to expect.

In the process of reorganizing, restructuring, and creating a system more compatible with the changing environment, Cooperative Extension is smaller, weaker, and more vulnerable than years
ago (Harriman & Daugherty, 1992 and Graf, 1993). Graf (1993)
stated while the health of an organization cannot be measured by
size alone, whether it is growing or declining is a good indicator.
Employees working in Cooperative Extension would not be alarmed
with the statistics of today to those of previous years. For example:

- What impact are programs making on the economic vitality,
environmental quality, and human development of this nation?
- How many fewer agents and program assistants do we have?
- How many fewer faculty are providing research for our
program?
- What resources are available for program delivery, travel,
and technology?
- How many fewer clientele are impacted by our programs?
- How many states and counties have either threatened, cut,
or eliminated Cooperative Extension?

In the face of these diminished resources:

- How many counties have experienced a reduced need for
Extension programs, or a reduced demand from clientele?

- How many staff members have simply spread themselves thinner, handling more subject matter with fewer resources?
- How many program assistants are doing what agents used to do? (p.30)

Graf (1993) suggested that Cooperative Extension must change its mode of operation to be able to compete and survive in today's society. Cooperative Extension staff can no longer work with the same tools provided 50 years ago.

IMPACT OF DOWNSIZING

Brockner (1988) presented a conceptual model that focused on the factors he believed moderate the reactions of survivors to coworkers' layoff.

> First, layoffs have the potential to engender a variety of psychological states in survivors. The survivors may experience job insecurity, positive inequity, anger, and even relief. In reference to this list, which by no means is complete, all reactions are not aversive. Second, the psychological states that layoffs evoke have the potential to affect survivors' work behaviors and attitudes. In addition, positive inequity could produce a significant boost in work motivation. (p.215)

The surviving employees, who believed their output to be less than that of the laid-off workers, may in fact increase their inputs. On the other hand, survivors who perceived the layoffs to be unfair may reduce their productivity and/or sabotage the organization in another way.

Job insecurity, positive inequity, and anger could lead to decreased organizational commitment and job satisfaction for survivors, stated Brockner (1988). Survivors could lose interest in their jobs, when they feel insecure them. Some of them become competitive believing they need to out perform their co-workers to remain employed.

> First, hiring freezes may have long-term negative consequences for an organization's ability to recruit good candidates; intermittent hiring freezes can signal that a business is in deep trouble or has potential problems with job insecurity.

Second, hiring freezes can significantly shift the age and experience distributions in an organization. Fewer and fewer young
people are hired into junior positions; there is less inflow of new
ideas and new perspectives; and there is no bottom-up mechanism
for retooling and reeducating older workers.

Third, hiring freezes may have a chilling effect on organizational
commitment to increasing diversity. Because women and minori-
ties are often disproportionately represented in the junior rank
organizations, organizational progress in building a diverse work
force can be significantly wiped out by hiring freezes (p. 147).

Feldman (1996) stated while cutting back on hiring may help a
firm that is stagnant or declining, organizational-wide hiring freezes
may be counter-productive. He further stated that even though a
firm might be undergoing restructuring or downsizing, it should
still provide sufficient guidance, counseling, and mentoring for
new hires (Feldman, 1996).

Over the past, it was believed that downsizing would increase
the productivity of American companies. However, downsizing
often fails to achieve what companies set out to accomplish even
though laying off people saves money (Cameron, 1994 and Lee,
1997). Stamps (1996) quoted AMA's statistics on downsizing,

Only 47 percent of the companies who reported work force reductions since 1990 realized any increase in operating profit within a
year following the reductions. Long-term (more than one year
after the cuts) only 46 percent reported increased profits. Only
one-third of the cost-cutting firms reported an increase in worker
productivity within a year after the cuts.

The tactics used to downsize removes the wrong people, levels,
or function from companies, stated Rubach (1995). In a survey conducted by an outplacement firm (Right Associated) in 1990, 74 percent of senior managers in downsized companies said that morale,
trust, and productivity suffered after downsizing (Henkoff, 1990
and Rubach, 1995). The Society for Human Resource Management
survey reported that more than half of the 1,468 firms surveyed
either made no change in employee productivity or it deteriorated
after downsizing (Henkoff, 1990 and Rubach, 1995). In another poll

conducted yearly since 1990 by the American Management Association's member companies, it was reported in 1996 that less than half of the companies which reduced work force had an increase in productivity, less than one third increased productivity (Lee, 1997). The survey also reported that 35 percent of the respondents increased turnover and 72 percent had a decrease in morale (Lee, 1997).

Most change efforts are doomed because management does not provide timely and accurate information to their employees. Richardson and Denton (1996) stated that when employees learn of changes in their organization from outsiders, failure of the efforts are bound to occur. According to Caudron (1996), when employees hear about an impeding merger, they lose trust in the organization, even though high level mergers are rarely announced to employees ahead of time. She quoted Ron Schaefer, a partner in an organizational consulting firm in Brookline, New Hampshire, "When trust is broken, communication stops, people don't talk about problems, the problems don't get addressed, productivity falls, and customer service declines. Until management restores trust, any initiatives designed to correct these problems are looked at unfavorably" (p. 20).

Constant change in organizations results in an uncertain and sometimes less promising future for employees. Researchers believed it is crucial that employees are given the tools to cope with change (Demers, Forrer, Leibowitz, and Cahill, 1996). If employees do not know how they fit into the new schema, their level of performance tended to decline (Bushel, 1996).

RESEARCH STUDIES AND CAREER DEVELOPMENT

Employees who had the right attitude and believe they were responsible for their own development, thrive and survive the turmoil of downsizing, stated Fox (1996). These employees responded to change in the workplace by developing their own career insurance (Fox, 1996).

Both Cameron (1994) and Hirsh (1987) stated little attention has been given to assist employees in developing their careers under sustained conditions of diminished resources. Feldman (1996) offered five sets of strategies to help employees manage their own careers when the opportunities of advancement are diminished, due to downsizing. They included:

- increasing internal mobility;
- seeking out additional training;
- maintaining technical excellence;
- sustaining outstanding performance by maintaining high levels of productivity and work effectiveness; and
- demonstrating team-oriented behavior (p. 151).

In addition, Feldman (1996) provided eight ways organizations might reorient their career management efforts in a downsizing environment.

> First, organizations need to shift their focus from managing short-term responses to layoffs to developing better long-term programs for managing careers in a downsized environment (Noer, 1993). Second, organizations will have to make exerted efforts to break out of the cycle of successive rounds of layoffs and the ensuing problems that each round of layoffs has for survivors (Brockner et al., 1993). Third, organizations need to shift gears from designing career management programs based on opportunities for growth and development. Fourth, not surprisingly, employees loyalty to corporations undergoing successive restructurings and downsizing is low; it is difficult for employees to feel committed to some organization whose continued existence is in doubt (Hirsh, 1987). As a result, the traditional tactics of trying to build corporate loyalty through orientation and socialization programs may be less likely to succeed (Noer, 1993). Fifth, for many large organizations, large-scale, formal training and development programs are the keystone of their career development activities. However, since downsizing almost always takes a major cut through staff support services, downsizing organizations have to become more judicious in how training and career development dollars are spent. Sixth, concentrating on a merit-based reward system helps to promote more effective career development. Seventh, when monetary rewards are unavailable, managers in downsizing firms might have to be more generous in their use of rewards such as praise to motivate performance. Finally, (eighth), when faced with external threats, organizations need to become more innovative and proactive in response to environment changes (p. 155).

According to Feldman (1996), organizations should modify the type of career development activities during the different stages of the employee's career. He stated, new hires should be provided with a variety of job assignments. This gives them an opportunity to both perform new tasks and to develop new skills (Feldman, 1996).

Feldman (1996) stated mid-career employees probably were affected by corporate restructuring the most. In downsized organizations, there are fewer positions for promotion and the mid-career employees have greater obstacles in keeping their current job, stated Feldman (1996). Firms can facilitate the career development of these employees by:

- periodic skill development;
- retraining and cross-training; and
- insuring middle-aged workers that they will not be disportionately targeted for layoffs or disportionately excluded from retraining programs (p. 148).

Since early retirement has been used by many organizations as an alternative to layoffs, Feldman (1996) suggested transition programs should be in place during downsizing. Employees who anticipate retirement should be given pre-retirement counseling by the organization at an earlier age Feldman (1996) said. "Next, 'open windows' programs which encourage older workers to take early retirement have to be carefully designed and closely monitored. Third, organizations can make better use of their recent retirees after their formal retirement" (p. 150). For instance, retirees can be given the option of working on special assignment, additional months after retirement, or part-time for a specified number of years (Feldman, 1996).

MANAGING CHANGE

Lehrer (1997) believed one of the ways of coping with a decline in employee morale and productivity is to acknowledge that employees do have some concerns that should be addressed. He stated, "Once the downsizing has been completed an organization needs to pay attention to what is on people's minds:

1. Have the goals of the organization changed?
2. Now that the agency has less staff, will roles and responsibilities change?

3. Will the company be required to issue the same number of reports, or will expected outputs be scaled back accordingly?
4. How can the company expect more with less staff if nothing else in the organization changes?
5. What does the future hold for me?" (p.16)

The above list represented a sample of some of the questions employees would like answered according to Lehrer (1997).

A four phase model was developed by Lehrer (1997) from dialogue of students who had been impacted by downsizing. The model discussed recurring effects of downsizing which Lehrer (1997) thought organizational leaders needed to recognize and deal with in order to lessen the pain of restructuring. They are:

- Phase 1 - **Downsizing Is Imminent**
- Phase II - **Downsizing Is Implemented**
- Phase III - **Downsizing Aftermath**
- Phase IV - **Renewal** (p.16)

In the first phase there are rumors about a possible streamlining of the organization. The disbelief and lack of communication among staff and employer results in a state of denial by staff. According to Lehrer (1997), when the staff realizes that downsizing is imminent, morale and productivity decline and trust in the organization is lost.

In the next phase, after downsizing is implemented, there is a continued drop in productivity and morale. Although the employees are somewhat relieved, they are still fearful because they knew that their job security is no longer apropos (Lehrer, 1997).

In the third phase, the remaining employees try to pick up the pieces, stated Lehrer (1997). These employees make attempts to regroup and perform their duties, but the restructuring has changed their role and responsibilities.

The renewal phase is where the survivors try to contribute to the functions of the organization. In this last phase the morale and productivity improves somewhat stated Lehrer (1997). Therefore, it is important that management makes adjustments in the operation. They should be especially aware of how the remaining employees are treated (Lehrer, 1997).

Borucki and Barnett (1990) agreed that organizational performance and effectiveness are ultimately impacted by how the victims of downsizing are treated. Brockner (1987) stated the guilt experienced by the survivors may cause their productivity to increase. In fact, recent research indicated that massive downsizing is frequently followed by increased productivity and quality, stated Berenbein (1986). Borucki and Barnett (1990) cited Kissler's study on ten General Electric plant closings in which he found productivity increased due to:

- a belief that hard work can reverse the decision;
- an act of defiance to show the decision was wrong;
- a way to "cleanse" a spotty work record; and
- wanting to avoid facing the realities of closing (p. 38).

Lehrer (1997) highlighted some strategies that leaders can use to negate the impact of downsizing:

1. Keep everyone informed about organizational change.
2. Develop up-front communication plans.
3. Clarify objectives and define strategic goals.
4. Provide opportunities for input at all levels.
5. Establish a corporate culture that values people and encourages collaboration.
6. Meet the challenge of restructuring by encouraging innovation and experimentation.
7. Provide assistance and support for coping with change (p. 19).

Corning, Inc., a Fortune 500 technology company, implemented a change management tool to help prevent or at least minimize the destructive cycle associated with change. The plan provided "employee counseling services, ways to cope with stress and change, self-assessment tools, and a focus on new employees and company relationships" (Demers et. al., 1996). The plan objectives were to:

1. Maximize the positive and minimize the impact of re-engineering on remaining employees.
2. Reduce the trauma of downsizing.
3. Facilitate a motivating environment to remobilize and revitalize remaining employees.
4. Provide a vehicle to plan for, respond to, and cope with change (p. 23).

The Human Resources Department of Corning, Inc., along with several outside consultants, developed "Exercise for Managing

Change," a self-directed tool kit, as a guide for their Human Resource and line managers to help with the transition to change. Even though feedback from this tool was positive, Corning's management discovered that it does not completely address all the issues involved with change. However, employee morale and productivity did improve when the tool kit was implemented according to Demers et al., (1996).

Rubach (1995) offered some suggestions which organizations can follow in order to have greater productivity, better quality, more flexibility, and higher profits after downsizing. They are to:

- not downsize for the sake of downsizing;
- keep quality intact;
- pay attention to remaining employees; and
- follow a new employment contract (p. 24).

Under this new contract, Rubach (1995) stated that responsibilities will be shared by both the employer and the employees. With shared responsibilities, the employees will be given:

- work that is important and interesting;
- control over both their work and careers;
- the freedom and resources to perform their work;
- pay that reflects their contributions to the organization; and
- the training they need to continue their employment (p.23).

This contract allowed the employees to be a valuable asset to the company as opposed to something that can be discarded. Rubach (1995) reiterated Harris' (1994) statement, "If organizations do not pay enough attention to cross level effects of downsizing, then their ability to efficiently transform inputs into outputs is seriously diminished."

Trahant and Burke (1996) provided a survey for assessing whether an organization is ready for change and how to help employees overcome their resistance to change. They agreed with other researchers in that "to be successful, change must be implemented at two levels: transformational and transactional" (Trahant and Burke, 1996). Both are based on the Burke-Litwin model which involves an organization's mission, strategy, vision, and culture at the transformational level and any system that facilitates peoples' work at the transactional level. In order for companies to implement successful change efforts, they need to be able to identify and deal with why a change is necessary. By using a change-management assessment instrument similar to Trahant and Warner's (1996) "Lay of the Land," companies can view the organizations' characteristics and how it works. The survey, "Lay of the Land," examined, the following areas: external environment, management values and practices, organizational culture, organizational structure, organizational systems, work climate, and performance (Trahant and Burke, 1996).

STRATEGIES FOR CHANGE IN EXTENSION

Extension has been challenged to change the way it does business in order to survive in the twenty-first century. The slashed budgets, taxpayer revolts, and federal cutbacks of the 1980's have moved into the 1990's. As a provider of both adult and youth education, White (1988) stated, "Extension must compete for existing program dollars, while at the same time doing more with less." The organization will no longer be able to operate as they did in the past. Both human and financial resources needed to be redirected, according to Pfeiffer (1989). Harriman and Daugherty stated, "The challenge is to chart a course compatible with the changing environment and drop programs and activities that deal with obsolete situations".

Since Cooperative Extension was established in 1914, the mode of program delivery was always county-based. Today's Extension clients are more knowledgeable and have a greater access to information. Extension staff must be able to provide greater in-depth information in their educational programs. In addressing high priority societal issues related to the environment, nutrition and health, waste management, and youth at risk, Extension staff need to be specialized. However, most county budgets can not support a number of specialized agents.

Cooperative Extension administrators in Nebraska explored methods to gain greater efficiency to be able to serve their clients with quality education and programs.

> This exploration resulted in developing multi county Extension programming units (EPUs) to replace single-county programs. The program units were designed to increase the Extension agents' role as an educator within a specialized area and create a situation in which agents could be more proactive in responding to critical issues (p. 17).

Graf (1993) stated Extension must face the fact that new sources of revenue are required to provide needed educational programs. Government funding was no longer adequate enough to support the level of programs from Extension needed by the communities. Graf (1993) stated, "Extension will need to look more closely at fee structures, grants, contracts with other agencies, private funding, and other nontraditional support to maintain a viable Extension System." He further stated, "If we only respond with more strategic planning, more reorganization, more regionalization, and more reports, we won't survive until the year 2000.

READINGS AND REFERENCES

Armstrong-Strassen, M. & Latack, J. C. (1992). Coping with work-force reduction: The effects of layoff exposure on survivors'reactions. *Proceedings of the Annual Meeting of the Academy of Management,* 207–211.

Berenbeim, R. E. (1986). *Company Programs to Ease the Impact of Shutdowns* , New York, NY: The Conference Board, Inc.

Borucki, C., & Barnett, C. (1990). Restructuring for self-renewal: Navistar international corporation. *Academy of Management Executive,* 4(1), 36–49.

Brockner, J. (1988). The effects of work layoffs on survivors: Research, theory, and practice. *Research in Organizational Behavior,* 10, 213–255.

Burack, E. H. & Singh, R. S. (1995). The new employment relations compact. *The Journal of The Human Resource Planning Society,* 18(1), 12–19.

Cascio, W. F. (1993). Downsizing: What do we know? What have we Learned? *Academy of Management Executive,* 7(1), 95–104.

Caudron, S. (1996). Rebuilding employee trust. *Training & Development,* 50(8), 18–21.

Demers, R., Forrer, S. E., Leibowits, Z., & Cahill, C. (1996). Commitment to change. *Training & Development,* 35(2), 203–216.

Feldman, D. C. (1996). Managing careers in downsizing firms. *Human Resource Management,* 35(2), 145–161.

Henkoff, R. (1990). Cost cutting: How to do it right. *Fortune,* 121(8), 40–49.

Henkoff, R. (1990). Cost cutting: How to do it right. *Fortune,* 121(8), 40–49.

Kuttner, R. (1993). Talking marriage and thinking one-night stand. *Business Week*, October 18.

Lee, C. (1997). Trust me. *Training,* 34(1), 28–37.

Lehrer, S. (1997). Effectively coping with downsizing. A four-phrase model. *The Government Accountants Journal*, 45(4), 16–19.

Levine, G. H. (1978). Organizational decline and cutback management. *Public Administration Review*, 38, 316–325.

Reece, B. (1996). The impact of communication on employee relation to organizational change. A case study. *Masters Abstracts International,* 34(2), 469. (University Microfilm No. AAC 1376288).

Richardson, P. & Denton, D. K. (1996). Communicating change. *Human Resource Management*, 35(2), 203–216.

Roach, S. S. (1996). The hollow ring of the productivity revival. *Harvard Business Review*, 74(6), 81–89.

Rubach, L. (1995). Downsizing How quality is affected as companies shrink: *Quality Progress,* 28(4), 23–25.

Whetten, D. A. (1980). Sources, responses, and effects of organizational decline, In J. R. Kimberly, R. H. Miles and Associates (Eds.), *The Organizational Life Cycle,* (pp. 342–374). San Francisco, CA: Josey-Boss Publishers.

Winston James, T. A. & Li-Ping Tang, T. (1996). Downsizing and the impact on survivors-A matter of justice. *Employment Relations Today*, 23(2), 33–41.

CHAPTER 3

Methodology

The purpose of this study is to gain qualitative insights on the impact downsizing has on employee morale and productivity: implications for leadership training (with special reference to Cooperative Extension). The expectation was to learn about employee perception of the job environment in light of downsizing. Drawing from these perceptions the researcher made inferences for future training and improvement. The research design, development of instruments, data collection techniques and analysis, and selection of subjects will be presented and discussed in this chapter.

POPULATION

The population of this study consisted of 58 employees who worked in Extension county offices and were part of the downsizing process. Two states, California and Illinois, were included in the study. These states were chosen because the researcher had prior knowledge of downsizing in California and the state of Illinois also experienced extensive downsizing. The researcher was interested in whether downsizing had a similar impact on employees in different regions. Funding for Cooperative Extension is derived from three sources, federal, state, and county. The way the funding is received will ultimately determine how employees are affected by downsizing.

A letter (see Appendix A) was mailed to each States' Personnel Department to request a list of employees and addresses and to ask permission to do the study. The number of staff working in county offices was 444 (obtained from a directory search - DANR.UCOP.edu) in California and 253 (mailed by William T. McNamara, Personnel Director) in Illinois.

SAMPLE

The researcher initially wanted to study all employees working in county offices, but specific employees (educators, unit educators, and unit educator assistants) were targeted for downsizing in Illinois. All employees in California had the potential of being downsized. Since there are no rules that governed the sample size, a 20% random sample was chosen to provide richness to the study. "Information richness is often the most important factor in the selection of samples. Because the selection of participants serves the purposes of an inquiry that often changes as it progresses, the numbers and types of participants involved in a study are often fluid," suggested Bradley (1993). The samples were as follows:

- In California, a total of 88 county employees consisting of 78 advisors, paraprofessionals, and clerical support in agriculture, home economics, and 4-H; 10 were County Directors.
- In Illinois, a total of 51 county employees consisting of 32 Extension Educator, Extension Unit Educators, and Unit Educator Assistants in agriculture, home economics, and youth development; 19 were Center Chairs and/or Unit Leaders.

The sample population was mailed October and November, 1997 a Manson's Workplace Inventory Analysis (Appendices B and C), an Informed Consent Document (Appendix D), and a demographic sheet (Appendix E) with a self-addressed stamp return envelope. Bogdan and Biklen (1998) stated, "two issues dominate traditional official guideline of ethics in research with human subjects: informed consent and the protection of subjects from harm. These guidelines attempt to insure that:

1. Subjects enter research projects voluntarily, understanding the nature of the study and the dangers and obligations that are involved.
2. Subjects are not exposed to risks that are greater than the gains they might derive" (p. 43).

An application for review was submitted to the Graduate School Review Board for approval before proceeding with the study, to assure the rights of human subjects. Approval was granted October 10, 1997 (see Appendix F).

The researcher used Dillman's total design method (TDM) to maximize the return of the inventory (Dillman, 1977). Dillman (1977) stated the process of getting prospective respondents to complete questionnaires in an honest manner and return them can be viewed as a "social exchange." "The theory of social exchange, the tenets of which have been notably developed by Homans, Blau, and Thibaut and Kelley, asserts that the actions of individuals are motivated by the return these actions are expected to bring and, in fact, usually do bring from other" (Dillman, 1977). According to Dillman (1977), "There are three things that must be done to maximize survey response: minimize the costs for responding, maximize the rewards for doing so, and establish trust that those rewards will be delivered." A follow-up postcard was mailed three weeks after the initial mailing and again one month later

Table 3.1 Inventories Distributed to and Returned from County Extension Staff

	Distributed	Returned	
	n	n	%
California			
Unknown		4	12
Advisor	44	20	45
Paraprofessional	20	5	25
Clerical	14	1	7
County Director	10	3	30
TOTAL	**88**	**33**	**38**
Illinois			
Educator	15	8	53
Unit Educator	4	3	75
Unit Educator Asst.	13	7	42
Center Chair	4	1	25
Unit Leader	15	9	60
TOTAL	**51**	**28**	**55**

(Appendix G). Table 3.1 shows a cross-section of the distribution and return rate by subjects of the inventory.

DESCRIPTION OF RESEARCH DESIGN
AND DATA ANALYSIS

Qualitative research methods were employed (an administered inventory and semi-structured individual interviews) as multiple source documentation. Van Maanen (1979) described qualitative methods as "an umbrella term covering an array of interpretive techniques which seek to describe, decode, translate, and otherwise come to terms with the meaning, not frequency, of certain more or less naturally occurring phenomena in the social world" (p. 520). Patton (cited in Bradley, 1993) and Whitt (1991) stated qualitative methods are considered best for achieving in-depth understanding of complex organizations and processes. According to Whitt (1991), "Studies of process ask how something happens and portray the dynamics of action and change, including the perceptions, experiences, and interactions of people involved in the process." The data collected was descriptive in that it will take the form of words in the written results. Even though some quantitative data will be presented, the written results has quotations from the data to illustrate and substantiate the presentation. "While qualitative data tends to probe enough to get the meaning events have for those who experience them," stated Leedy (1993), "it does not imply that qualitative inquiry makes no use of quantification" (p. 142).

In utilizing interviews, the researcher will be able to obtain the respondents' perspectives and perceptions. "The purpose of interviewing is to find out what is in or on someone else's mind," stated Patton (as cited in Bradley, 1993). The meaning derived from the data is essential because Bogdan and Biklen (1995) stated, "Meaning provides the bases of how people see their lives (p.7)." "Interviews are used to gather information regarding an individuals experiences and knowledge; his or her opinions, beliefs, and feelings; and demographics data" (Best and Kahn, 1998, p. 255). Interviews can also confirm and expand the information already obtained during the study because they allow the researcher to analyze and interpret what is heard, and if needed to probe for additional information (Whitt, 1991. p. 411).

Instrumentation

The instrumentation (Appendices B and C) was designed to obtain the data necessary to answer the research questions set forth in Chapter 1. An inventory analysis matrix was used for categorizing the instrument item (Appendix H). A pilot study was conducted on the instruments for clarity and to find out the length of time needed for completion. Letters asking for permission to pilot the instrument in Kansas county offices are in Appendix I. The Informed Consent Document (Appendix D) provides: (1) what the research is designed to study, (2) what the subject will be expected to do, and (3) a guarantee of confidentiality along with the names, addresses, and phone numbers of the researcher and the chairperson of the committee.

The demographic sheet (Appendix E) contains five questions that related to the research. They were: (1) gender, (2) age, (3) educational background, (4) years of experience with employer, and (5) job title. The gender and job title were important to assure that all employees were represented in the study. The age, educational background, and years of service were warranted to determine if differences occur in perception due to background.

The Manson's Workplace Environment Analysis Inventory was designed using a closed-question format. In Part I, the respondents were presented with various alternative response options from a list of stated options. The researcher also provided for unanticipated responses by providing an "other" category for some statements (Best and Kahn, 1998, p. 300). Part II utilized a Likert-type scale whereby respondents had five responses ranging from "strongly agree" to "strongly disagree" as their choice.

Open-ended questions were used in constructing the interview questions (Appendix J). This permitted a free response from the subjects and allowed them to answer in their own words. Best and Kahn (1998) stated, "An open-form question . . . is likely to provide greater depth of response. In fact, this penetration exploits the advantage of the interview in getting beneath-the-surface reactions" (p. 321).

Method of Triangulation

Multiple methods of data collection (triangulation) were employed to strengthen credibility of this study. Credibility is one of the four criteria used to establish the "trustworthiness" of qualitative data, stated Lincoln and Guba (1985). Denzin defined triangulation (as cited in Jick, 1979) as "The combination of methodologies in the study of the same phenomenon" (p.291). "Triangulation can also be achieved by collecting essentially the same data from different samples, at different times, and in different places," stated Borg and Gall (1989) (p.393). When studying human subjects, the data obtained may not accurately report the questions being studied. Van Maanen (1979) stated, "Data that consist of respondents' statements can be misleading because people are likely to knowingly or unknowingly put themselves and their institution or group in the best possible light." According to Borg and Gall (1989), the researcher can be more confident of the findings when using triangulation because the data can be replicated. Guba and Lincoln (1985) stated, "The techniques of triangulation is the third mode of improving the probability that findings and interpretations will be found credible" (p.305). To support the credibility of this study, data from different regional locations, geographic areas, and types of employees was collected and analyzed. Data from the inventories and interviews helped to strengthen the findings.

Data Analysis

Bradley (1998) stated, "The analytic process, in general, can be described as breaking down the data into smaller pieces by identifying meaningful units, grouping these together in categories, and developing relationships among the categories in such a way that patterns in the data are made clear." The data was categorized using a Workplace Analysis Matrix (see Appendix H) to answer the research questions that have guided this study. The research objectives were:

1. To determine whether the morale of employees can improve in a downsized organization.
2. To determine if the job performance of survivors can improve after downsizing.
3. To determine whether trust can be rebuilt after layoffs.

Marshall and Rossan wrote (as cited in Whitt, 1991), "Qualitative data analysis is the process of bringing order, structure, and meaning to the mass of collected data." Patton (as cited in Whitt,

1991) offered some guidelines to follow because there are no set formats to follow when writing qualitative research. He stated, "Reports of qualitative research require 'thick description,' or detailed descriptions of what was done and why, and the phenomena studied. The researcher reported verbatim quotations of the subjects interviewed and those who submitted additional comments. Secondly, "any report of qualitative research should be directed to its intended audience" (Whitt, 1991). The results from the data can be used to design leadership training programs for community based organizations such as Extension Services.

The categories that guided the study are: Morale, Survivor Job Security, and Trust (in the workplace). The items related to information which impacts how employees feel about their work environment are:

1. An ideal work environment should include the following:
   a. flexible scheduling
   b. input on assignments
   c. personal computers
   d. friendly co-workers
   e. other, please list
2. An ideal method for communicating anticipated downsizing to employees is:
   a. office memos
   b. employee meetings
   c. rumors
   b. the media
   e. other, please list
3. The following number of employees working in county offices have been promoted in the last 5 years.
   a. 1–3
   b. 3–6
   c. 6–9
   d. 10 or more
   e. unknown
4. The following number of employees working in county offices have been promoted in the last 10 years.
   a. 1–3
   b. 3–6
   c. 6–9

    d.   10 or more

    e.   unknown

5. My/employees' general response to an unfavorable performance evaluation is to:

    a.   work harder

    b.   ask for assistance

    c.   do nothing

    d.   sabotage the company in some way

    e.   other, please list

6. My/employees' general response to a positive performance evaluation is to:

    a.   work harder

    b.   work satisfactorily

    c.   slack off

    d.   expect advancement

    e.   other, please list

13. The program budget allows for employees to attend training workshops.

strongly agree, agree, neutral, disagree, and strongly disagree

The items that addressed Workplace Morale were:

7. I first heard about Cooperative Extension's plans to downsize by:

    a.   office memos

    b.   employee meetings

    c.   rumors

    d.   the media

    e.   other, please list

8. Rank the following employee incentives with 5 being extremely important and 1 being least important.

    ___merit increase

    ___promotion opportunities

    ___bonus

    ___empowerment

    ___other, please list

The remaining items were identified using the following code:

    SA = Strongly agree

    A = Agree

    N = Neutral (no knowledge)

    D = Disagree

    SD = Strongly disagree

9. Employees are able to advance within the Cooperative Extension System.
10. Management is consistent in their treatment of employees.
11. Released time is allowed for staff to attend professional/skill development workshops.
12. I/employees received a clearly written job description when employed by Cooperative Extension.
19. Support or assistance to perform my duties decreased after Cooperative Extension downsized their county offices.

The items devoted to Survivor Job Security were:
15. Management provides training to assist employees in performing their job.
16. Employees incentives encourage increased output.
17. Employees are able to perform at the same level as they did before Cooperative Extension downsized their county offices.
18. The employees' performance level decreased after Cooperative Extension downsized their county offices.
20. The technology provided by Cooperative Extension improved my job performance.

The items related to Trust (in the workplace) were:
14. Employees are given a verbal warning about unsatisfactory performance before receiving an unfavorable job evaluation.
21. Management provided timely and accurate information about their downsizing.
22. I am/employees are responsible only for duties listed on the written job description.
23. Trust can be rebuilt in organizations faced with downsizing.
24. Employees were informed of anticipated changes in Cooperative Extension by management before downsizing.
25. Management is fair in their treatment of employees.
26. My contributions to Cooperative Extension are appreciated by management.

The interview questions were written verbatim to add to the richness of the data.

READINGS AND REFERENCES

Best, J. W. & Kahn, J. V. (1998). *Research in Education* (8th ed.). Boston: Allyn & Bacon.

Bogdan, R. C. & Biklen, S. D. (1998). *Qualitative Research in Education* (3rd ed.). Boston: Allyn & Bacon.

Borg, W. R. & Gall, M. D. (1989). *Educational Research An Introduction* (5th ed.) New York: Longman

Bradley, J. (1993). Methodological issues and practices in qualitative research. *Library Quarterly*, 63(4), 431–449.

Dillan, d. A. (1978). (Ed.). *Mail and Telephone Surveys*. New York: John Wiley & Sons.

Leedy, P. D. (1993). Research methodology: Qualitative or quantitative? *Practical Research Planning and Design* (5th ed., pp. 137–147). New York: MacMillan.

Lincoln, Y. S. & Guba, E. G. (1985). *Naturalistic Inquiry*. Newbury Park, CA: Sage.

Van Maanen, J. (Ed.). Reclaiming qualitative methods for organizational research: A preface. *Administrative Science Quarterly*, 24(4), 520–526.

CHAPTER 4

Results of the Study Description, Analysis, and Interpretation

This study provides insight on the perception of the work environment for county employees impact by downsizing in Extension Services. The researcher proposes that when employees feel helpless in their environment, they are unable to perform at the level needed to do the job. Brockner, Grover, and Blonder (1988) write, "Workers are bound to worry about their own job security. Layoff-produced stress, in turn, has the potential to influence a variety of survivors'work-behavior and attitudes . . . Stress tends to reduce employees' involvement with their jobs and the organization (manifested by such outcomes as reduced productivity, greater absenteeism and turnover, and lower job satisfaction" (p.437). Or the employees' affective states and levels of productivity may be systematically altered, state Brockner, Davy, and Carter (1985). They state, "Their co-workers' dismissal may engender perceived job insecurity (i.e., anxiety) in the survivors. Consequently, the survivors may work harder in order to avoid meeting a similar fate".

In light of these premises, the study was pursued to find out how downsizing in Cooperative Extension affects job performance, employee morale, and trust. The researcher was concerned with issues of morale and productivity, while noting factors of advanced training and seniority in Cooperative Extension employment.

The inventory questions were categorized using the Workplace Analysis Matrix (Appendix H). The categories includes: information, morale, productivity, and trust. Items 1–6 and 13 were devoted to information which could impact how employees feel about their work environment and its affect on their performance. Items 7–12 and 19 are related to workplace morale; 15–18 and 20 to survivor job security; and items 14 and 21–26 to trust (in the workplace). Participants had a choice of marking multiple items.

DESCRIPTIVE PROFILE OF PARTICIPANTS IN THIS STUDY

The sample in this study is comprised of fifty-eight subjects (42%) who returned a completed inventory. There was a total of twenty-one males, thirty-six females, and one unspecified gender. The California sample consisted of nine males, twenty-one females, and one unknown. The Illinois sample had twelve males and fifteen females. These participants resulted in a study sample which was thirty-five percent males, sixty-three percent females, and two percent unknown (see Table 4.1). For the purpose of this study, the participants and data will be reported separately because samples studied are not identical. No attempt will be made to compare the two states for this reason.

The California participants'lowest age range was 21–30 and the highest was 50 or more. Forty-two percent were within fifty or more year old range (see Table 4.2). The range of their educational background was high school to a terminal degree. A majority (32%) of the participants had a master's degree plus additional hours (see Table 4.3). The years of experience with Cooperative Extension was less than one year to sixteen or more years. Most of the sample (61 %) had at least eleven years of experience with Cooperative Extension (see Table 4.4). The gender of participants consisted of 68% female, 29% male, and 3% unknown (see Table 4.5). Personal data of staff is found in Table 4.6.

In Illinois, the participants'lowest age range was twenty-one to thirty and the highest was forty-one to fifty year old. The majority (37%) were between the forty-one to fifty age range (see Table 4.7). Their educational background was four years of college to a terminal degree. Most of the participants (41%) had a master's degree or a master's degree plus additional hours (see Table 4.8). The years of experience range from one to five years category to sixteen or more year range. Forty-eight percent of the participants had sixteen

Table 4.1 Summary Data of Participants

Gender	#	Percentage
Male	21	36.21%
Female	36	62.07%
Unknown	1	1.72%
Total	58	100
Age		
0 > 21	0	0
21–30	6	10
31–40	10	17
41–50	20	34
50+	22	38
Unknown	1	2
Total	58	100
Schooling		
High School	1	1.72%
Bachelors	15	25.86%
Masters	16	27%
Masters plus	19	32.76%
Ph. D.	6	10.34%
Unknown	1	1.72%
TOTAL	58	100.00%
Years of Experience		
> 1 year	2	3.45%
1–5 years	11	18.97%
6–10 years	9	15.52%
11–15 Years	9	15.52%
16+	26	44.83%
Unknown	1	1.72%
TOTAL	58	100.00%

or more years of experience in Cooperative Extension and twenty-six percent had one to five years of experience (see Table 4.9). The gender of the participants consisted of 56% female and 44% male (see Table 4.10). Personal data of employees can be found in Table 4.11.

Table 4.2

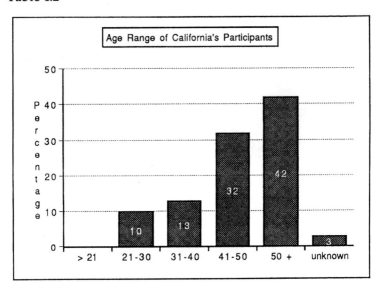

Table 4.3

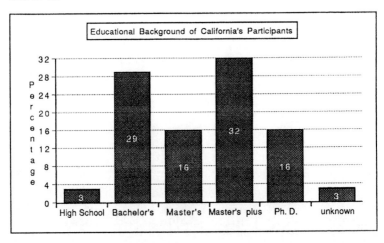

Table 4.4

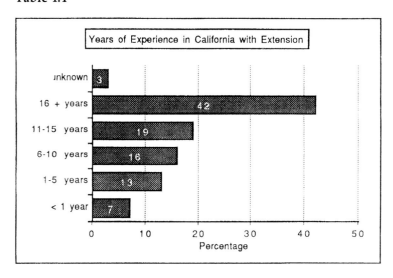

Table 4.5

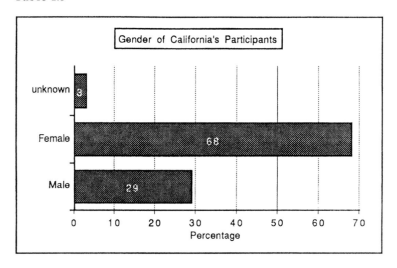

Table 4.6 Personal Data of California Participants

Participant #	Gender	Age	Educational Background	Years Experience
1	Female	41–50	Master plus	16 or more
2	Male	50 +	Master	16 or more
3	Female	41–50	Master plus	11–15 years
4	Female	41–50	Master plus	6–10 years
5	Female	50 +	Bachelor	10 or more
6	Male	31–40	Ph. D.	< 1 year
7	Female	41–50	Master	16 or more
8	Female	50 +	Master	1–5 years
9	Female	50 +	Bachelor	6–10 years
10	Male	50 +	Ph. D.	16 or more
11	Female	41–50	Bachelor	< 1 year
12	Female	41–50	Master plus	16 or more
13	Male	50 +	Master plus	16 or more
14	Female	41–50	Master plus	16 or more
15	Female	50 +	Bachelor	11–15 years
16	Male	21–30	Bachelor	1–5 year
17	Female	21–30	Bachelor	1–5 year
18	Female	41–50	Ph. D.	16 or more
19	Female	21–30	High School	11–15 years
20	Female	50 +	Master plus	16 or more
21	Male	41–50	Master	16 or more
22	Male	50 +	Master	11–15 years
23	Female	41–50	Master plus	6–10 years
24	Female	31–40	Master	11–15 years
25	unknown	unknown	unknown	unknown
26	Male	50 +	Bachelor	6–10 years
27	Female	50 +	Bachelor	16 or more
28	Female	31–40	Bachelor	1–5 years
29	Female	31–40	Master plus	6–10 years
30	Female	50 +	Ph. D.	11–15 years
31	Male	50 +	Ph. D.	16 or more

Table 4.7

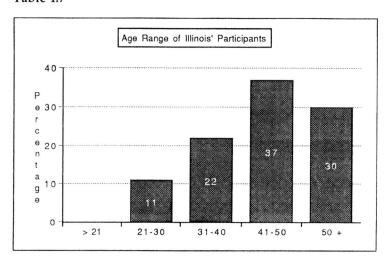

Table 4.8

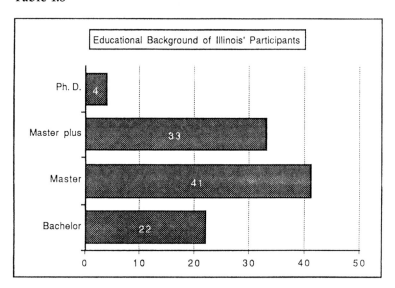

Table 4.9

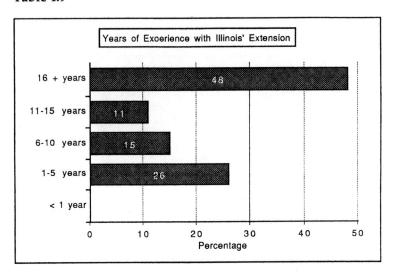

Table 4.10

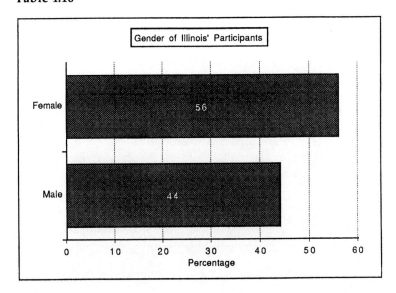

Table 4.11 Personal Data of Illinois' Participants

Participant #	Gender	Age	Educational Background	Years Experience
1	Female	41–50	Master	16 or more
2	Male	41–50	Master plus	11–15 years
3	Male	50 +	Master plus	16 or more
4	Male	31–40	Master	11–15 years
5	Female	41–50	Master	6–10 years
6	Female	50 +	Bachelor	6–10 years
7	Female	21–30	Bachelor	1–5 years
8	Female	41–50	Master	11–15 years
9	Female	31–40	Master	16 or more
10	Female	41–50	Master	1–5 years
11	Female	31–40	Bachelor	1–5 years
12	Female	21–30	Bachelor	1–5 years
13	Female	21–30	Bachelor	1–5 years
14	Male	50 +	Master plus	16 or more
15	Female	41–50	Master plus	16 or more
16	Male	31–40	Master plus	16 or more
17	Female	41–50	Master plus	16 or more
18	Female	31–40	Master	1–5 years
19	Male	50 +	Master	16 or more
20	Male	50 +	Master plus	16 or more
21	Male	50 +	Master	6–10 years
22	Male	41–50	Master	1–5 years
23	Male	31–40	Master	16 or more
24	Male	50 +	Bachelor	16 or more
25	Female	50 +	Ph.D.	6–10 years
26	Female	41–50	Master	16 or more
27	Male	41–50	Master	16 or more
*28	Female	50 +	Master plus	16 or more

*No survey returned.

California

Item 1: An ideal work environment should include the following: Eighty-six percent (24) of staff employees selected flexible scheduling and input on assignments; 82% (23) personal computers

and friendly co-workers; and 36% (10) other as their choices of an
ideal work environment. The other choices they wrote included:
office space, supportive supervision, team work, quiet space, supportive administration, adequate funding, professional development, and adequate/support staff. Three of management (100%)
selected input on assignment and 2 (67%) office space, friendly co-
workers, and flexible scheduling as their choices of an ideal work
environment (see Table 4.12). They did not list any additional items.

Item 2: An ideal method for communicating anticipated downsizing to employees is:

Ninety-three percent (26) of the staff employees chose employee
meetings; 25% (7) other; and 11% (3) office memos as an ideal
method for communicating anticipated downsizing to employees.
The choices they listed were: personal and/or private meetings;
personal, direct, and decision choice conferences; personal consultation; and individual meetings. Three of management (100%)
selected employee meeting and 2 (67%) selected other as an ideal
method for communicating anticipated downsizing to employees
(see Table 4.13). They listed personal discussions, individual face
to face and group meetings as other choices.

Table 4.12

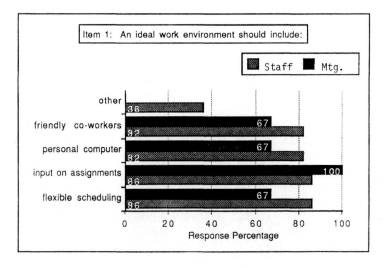

Table 4.13

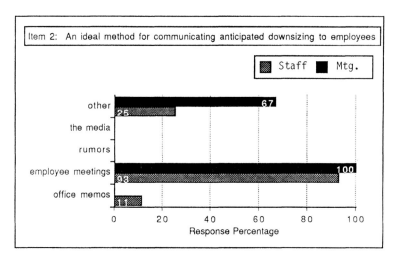

Item 2:   An ideal method for communicating anticipated downsizing to employees

Item 3: The following number of employees working in county offices have been promoted in the last 5 years.

The majority, fifty-six percent (15) of the staff employees did not know how many employees had been promoted in the last 5 years. Fifteen percent (4) selected the 10 or more category. Eleven percent (3) chose the 1–3 category and 7% chose the 6–9 category or stated none here. Four percent (1) of staff employees did not answer this item. One each of management (33.3%) selected equally the 1–3, 3–6, and 6–9 category for the number of employees promoted in the last 5 years (see Table 4.14).

Item 4: The following number of employees working in county offices have been promoted in the last 10 years.

Fifty-seven percent (16) of the staff employees did not know the number of employees working in county offices that have been promoted in the last 10 years. Eighteen percent (5) selected the 10 or more category. Eleven percent (3) chose the 1–3 category and 7% (2) selected the 3–6 category or did not answer this item. Two (67%) of management selected the 3–6 category and 1 (33%) the 10 or more category for the number of employees promoted in the last 10 years (see Table 4.15).

Table 4.14

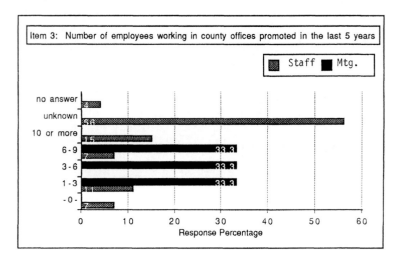

Item 5: My general response or employees'general response to an unfavorable performance evaluation is to:

Sixty-four percent (18) of the staff employee selected ask for assistance for their general response to an unfavorable performance evaluation. Thirty-six percent (10) chose work harder and 32% (9)

Table 4.15

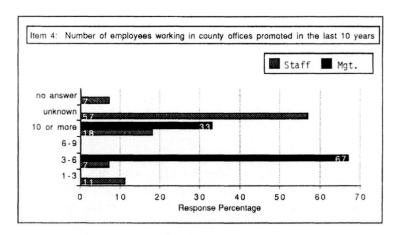

selected other. The other choices they listed are: get discouraged; write a better "Promotion Review" document; ask how to improve my evaluation; ask for specific actions needed to improve; I've never had one, (but) If I did, I expect to work collectively with my supervisor establishing goals; try again another year; non-applicable; concentrate on the work I find meaningful; and (I) have not encounter this; and clarify goals. Two (67%) of management selected ask for assistance and other for the way they felt employees reacted to an unfavorable performance evaluation. One (33) of management selected do nothing and work harder (see Table 4.16). Under the "do nothing" category one wrote in two question marks. The choices written for other are: depends on personality of individual, and grieve.

Item 6: My general response or employees'general response to a positive performance evaluation is to:

Forty-six percent (13) of the staff employees selected work harder as their general response to a positive performance evaluation. Thirty-six percent (10) chose expect advancement and 21% (6) selected work satisfactorily and other. Four percent (1) did not answer this item. The choices written for other included: become more focused, concentrate on the work I find meaningful, continue to maintain productivity, be more willing to support (the) organization, and work smarter. Two (67%) of management selected

Table 4.16

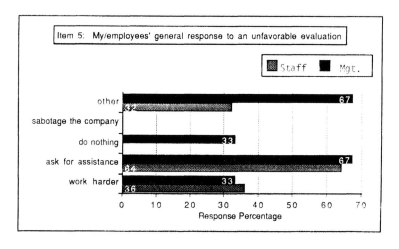

work harder and expect advancement for employees' general response to an unfavorable performance evaluation. One (33%) of management selected work satisfactorily and other for how they felt employees react to a positive performance evaluation (see Table 4.17). The choice listed is: focus on improvements.

Item 7: I first heard or employees were first notified about Cooperative Extension's plan to downsize by:

Twenty-five percent (7) of the staff employees selected employee meetings and other as to how they were notified about Cooperative Extension's plan to downsize. Twenty-one percent (6) of staff employees selected rumors and 18% (5) did not answer this item. Fourteen percent (4) of staff chose office memos and 4% (1) the media. The staff employees'other choices included: e-mail, newsletters, actions of administration, never heard this, and I haven't heard any information. Two staff employees (7%) wrote: have not heard. Three (100%) of management selected employee meetings as their choice of how employees were notified about Cooperative Extension's plan to downsize (see Table 4.18).

Item 8: Rank the following incentives in order of importance to employees with 5 being extremely important and 1 being least important.

Table 4.17

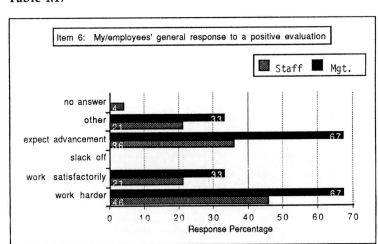

Table 4.18

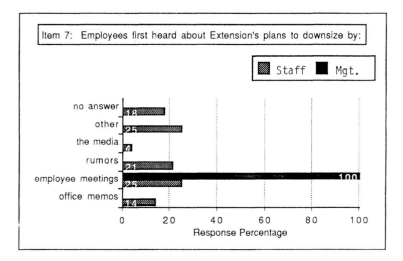

Item 7: Employees first heard about Extension's plans to downsize by:

When asked to rank employee incentives in the order of importance with 5 being extremely important and 1 being least important, both staff employees and management ranked *merit increase, promotion opportunities,* and *empowerment* relatively equal. It should be noted that several staff employees gave the same rank to some choices. *Bonus* and *other* receive a rank of two by staff employees. Management ranked these two categories 1.33 and 0.33 respectively (see Table 4.19). Staff employees wrote next to the *bonus* category the following: not an option in our county, non-applicable, and doesn't exist. Staff employees wrote the following under *other:* not listed; appreciation and value shown to employees; flexible scheduling; recognition; small thank you gift; question mark; part time employees; don't know; promotion that is TIMELY, not 8 months after submission; and adequate support staff and resources. The *other* category for management listed inclusion [make member part of (the) team].

The responses to Part II were:

1. strongly agree
2. agree
3. neutral (no knowledge)

Table 4.19

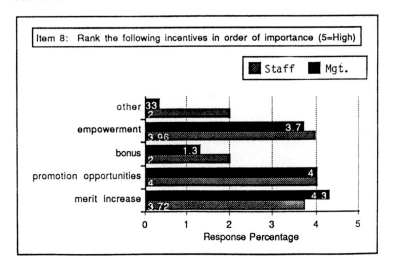

4. disagree
5. strongly disagree

Item 9: Employees are able to advance within the Cooperative Extension System.

Fifty-seven percent (16) of staff employees felt that employees could advance in Cooperative Extension and 3 (100%) of management felt it was possible. Twenty-four percent (7) of staff employees were in disagreement and 19% (5) had no knowledge of whether employees could advance in the Cooperative Extension System (see Table 4.20). A staff employee who disagreed commented: "I have a B S and I am working on a Master's (degree). I am a paraprofessional."

Item 10: Management is consistent in their treatment o employees or all employees are treated consistently by management.

The majority, fifty-three percent (15) of staff employees felt management was not consistent in their treatment of employees. However, 2 (67%) of management felt they treated all employees consistently. Twenty-five percent (7) of staff employees felt management was consistent in their treatment while 21% (6) had no

Table 4.20

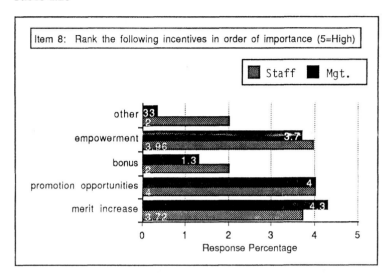

knowledge. One (33%) of management felt that they did not treat employees consistently (see Table 4.21).

Item 11: Released time is allowed for staff to attend professional/skill development workshops.

Eighty-six percent (24) of staff employees and 3 (100%) of management felt released time is allowed for staff to attend professional/skill development workshops. Seven percent (2) of staff disagree or had no knowledge of whether released time was allowed for workshops (see Table 4.22).

Item 12: I received or all employees are given a clearly written job description upon employment by Cooperative Extension.

Fifty percent (14) of staff felt they received clearly written job description when they were employed by Cooperative Extension. Two (67%) of management felt that employees are given a clearly written job description upon employment by Cooperative Extension. Thirty-six percent (10) of staff employees disagreed and 14% (4) had no knowledge of whether they got a clearly written job description when they were employed by Cooperative Extension. One staff employee who disagreed wrote, "I then reviewed and revised it." One (33%) of management did not think that all

Table 4.21

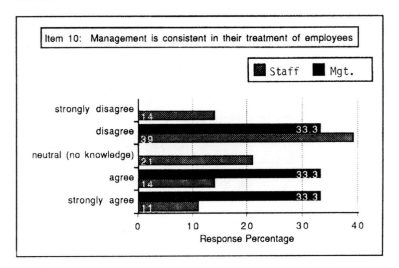

employee were given clearly written job descriptions upon employment by Cooperative Extension (see Table 4.23).

Item 13: The program budget allows for employees to attend training workshops.

Eighty-five percent (24) of staff employees and 3 (100%) of management agreed that the program budget allows for employees

Table 4.22

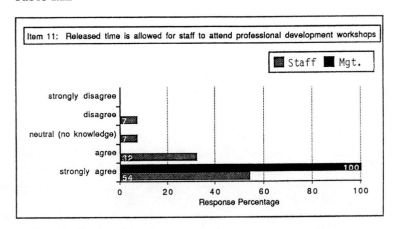

Table 4.23

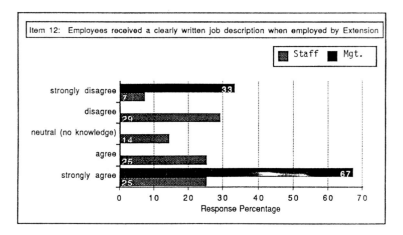

to attend training workshops. One of management who agreed wrote, "More is needed." Seven percent (2) of staff employees disagreed or had no knowledge of whether the program budget allowed for employees to attend training workshops (see Table 4.24). One staff who disagreed about the program budget allowing for employees to attend training workshops wrote, "Not enough money."

Table 4.24

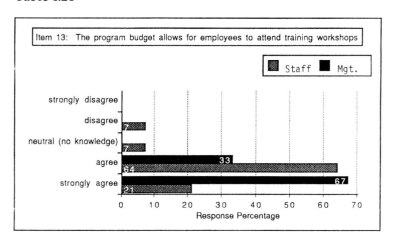

Item 14: Employees are given a verbal warning about unsatisfactory performance before receiving an unfavorable job evaluation.

Fifty-seven percent (16) of staff felt a verbal warning about unsatisfactory performance was given before an employee received an unfavorable job evaluation. However, only one (33%) of management agreed while, the other two (67%) felt that employees did not receive a verbal warning first. One of management who disagreed wrote, "Not often enough." Twenty-five percent (7) of staff employees had no knowledge and 18% (5) disagreed that employees were warned verbally before receiving an unfavorable job evaluation (see Table 4.25). One staff employee who disagreed wrote, "Lengthy review process means feedback process can be delayed by 1–3 years."

Item Item 15: Training is provided by management to assist employees in performing their job.

Both staff employees, seventy-eight percent (22) and two (67%) of management agreed that management provides training to assist employees in performing their job. One of management who agreed wrote, "It is getting better." Fourteen percent (4) of staff had no knowledge and 7% (2) felt management did not provide training to assist employees in performing their job. One (33%) of management disagreed that training is provided to employees to assist them in performing their job (see Table 4.26).

Item 16: Employee incentives encourages increased output.

Table 4.25

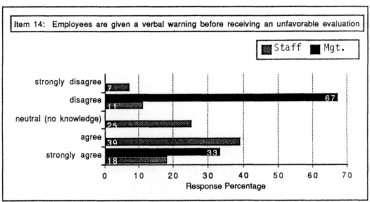

Table 4.26

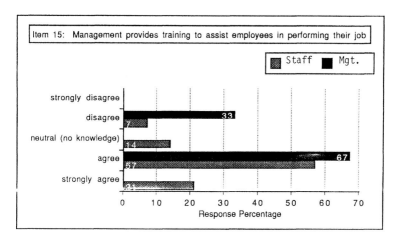

Fifty percent (14) of staff employees felt employee incentives encourage increased output. Only one (33.3%) of management felt employee incentives would increase output. Twenty-one percent (6) of staff employee had no knowledge or disagreed that employee incentives encourages increased output. Seven percent (2) of staff employee did not answer this item. One (33.3%) of management either had no knowledge or disagreed that employee incentives encourages increased output (see Table 4.27).

Item 17: Employees are able to perform at the same level as they did before Cooperative Extension downsized their county offices.

Half of staff employees, fifty percent (14) and the majority, sixty-seven percent (2) of management felt employees were not able to perform at the same level as they did before downsizing at county offices in Cooperative Extension. Twenty-one percent (6) of staff employee had no knowledge or agreed that employees could perform at the same level as they did before Cooperative Extension downsized their county offices. Seven percent (2) of staff employee did not answer this item. Thirty-three percent (1) of management felt employees could perform at the same level as they did before downsizing (see Table 4.28).

Item 18: The employees' performance level decreased after Cooperative Extension downsized their county offices.

Table 4.27

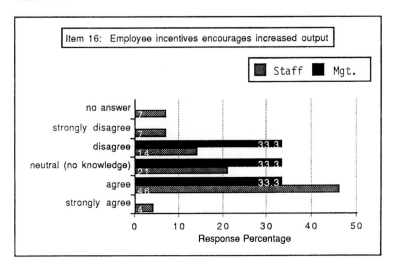

Staff employees were equally divided. Thirty-six percent (10) agreed and disagreed that employees' performance level decreased after Cooperative Extension downsized their county offices. Two (67%) of management disagreed that employees' performance level decreased after Cooperative Extension downsized their county

Table 4.28

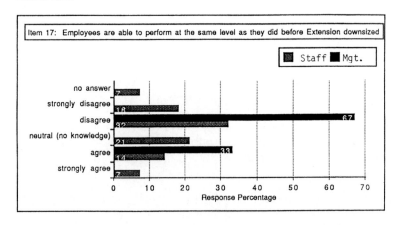

offices. However, one (33%) agreed. Twenty-one percent (6) of staff employees had no knowledge of whether employees' performance level decreased after downsizing (see Table 4.29). One staff employee who had no knowledge wrote, "(We) lost state level support." Another staff employee who disagreed wrote, "Never had any support!" Seven percent (2) of staff employees did not answer this item.

Item 19: Support or assistance provided by management decreased after Cooperative Extension's county offices downsized.

Fifty-seven percent (13) of staff employees and one (33%) of management felt support or assistance provided by management decreased after Cooperative Extension downsized their county offices. Thirty-two percent (9) of staff employees had no knowledge and 14% (4) disagreed that support or assistance by management decreased after Cooperative Extension downsized their county offices. One (33%) of management had no knowledge or disagreed that support or assistance provided by management decreased after Cooperative Extension downsized their county offices (see Table 4.30).

Item 20: The technology provided by Cooperative Extension improved my or employees' job performance.

The majority 74.5% (21) of staff and 3 (100%) of management felt technology provided by Cooperative Extension improved their

Table 4.29

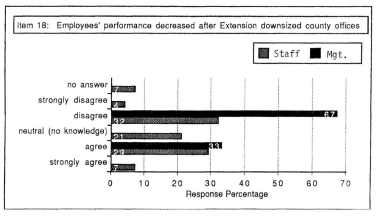

Table 4.30

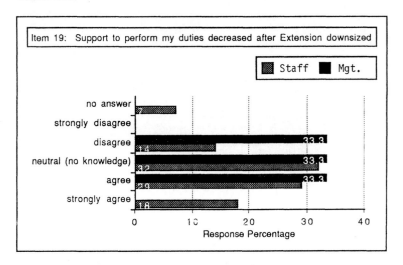

or employees' job performance. Twenty-two percent (6) of staff employees disagreed and 3.5% (1) had no knowledge of whether technology provided by Cooperative Extension improved their job performance (see Table 4.31). One staff employee who disagreed wrote, "I have purchased my own computer and work at home two days a week."

Item 21: Management provided timely and accurate information about their downsizing.

Only 32% (9) of staff employees felt management provided timely and accurate information about their downsizing. However, 2 (67%) of management felt that they did provide timely and accurate information about their downsizing. More staff employees, 43% (12) had no knowledge of whether management provided timely and accurate information about their downsizing. Twenty-five percent (7) of staff employee and one (33%) of management felt that management did not provide timely and accurate information about their downsizing (see Table 4.32). One staff employee who disagreed wrote, "I haven't heard anything."

Item 22: I am responsible or employees are responsible only for duties listed on the written job description.

Seventy-one percent (20) of staff employees and 2 (67%) of management felt that they or employees were responsible for

Table 4.31

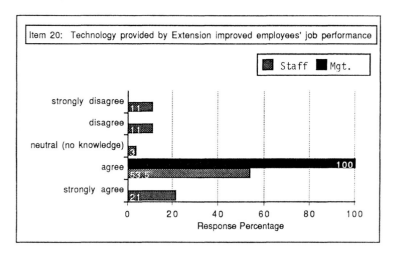

duties not listed on their job description. Twenty-five percent (6) of staff employees agreed they were responsible only for duties listed on their written job description. Eleven percent (2) of staff employees and one (33%) of management had no knowledge of whether employees were responsible for duties not listed on the job description (see Table 4.33).

Table 4.32

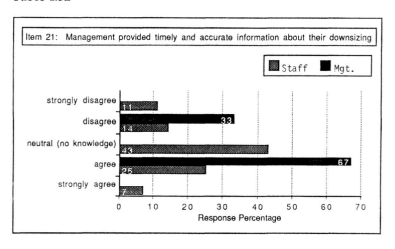

Table 4.33

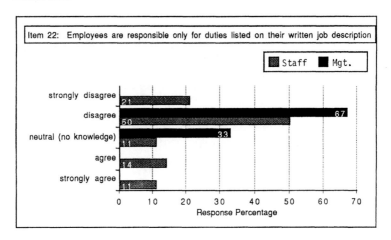

Item 23: Trust can be rebuilt in organizations faced with downsizing.

The majority of staff employees, 68% (19) and all 3 (100%) of management felt trust can be rebuilt in organizations faced with downsizing. Eighteen percent (5) of staff employees had no knowledge and 14% (4) disagreed that trust can be rebuilt in organizations faced with downsizing (see Table 4.34).

Item 24: Employees were informed of anticipated changes in Cooperative Extension by management before downsizing.

Fifty-seven percent (13) of staff employees and 2 (67%) of management agreed employees were informed of anticipated changes in Cooperative Extension by management before downsizing. One staff employee who agreed wrote, "Downsizing was handled by retirement incentives." Forty-three percent (12) of staff employees and one (33%) of management had no knowledge about whether employees were informed of anticipated changes in Cooperative Extension by management before downsizing. Four percent (1) of staff employees disagree or did not answer this item (see Table 4.35).

Item 25: Management is fair in their treatment of employees.

Thirty-nine percent (11) of staff employees felt management is fair in their treatment of employees. Two (67%) of management felt they are fair in their treatment of employees. Thirty-two percent (9) of staff employees had no knowledge and 29% (8) disagreed

Table 4.34

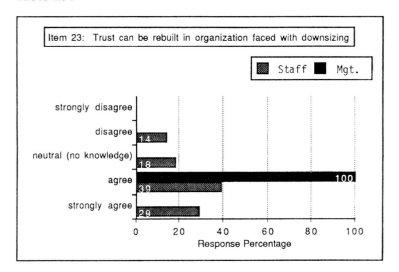

that management is fair in their treatment of employees. One (33%) of management felt they had no knowledge of whether they were fair in their treatment of employees (see Table 4.36). One staff employee who disagreed that management is fair in their treatment of employees wrote, "Not always."

Item 26: My contribution or employees'contributions to Cooperative Extension are appreciated by management.

Sixty-eight percent (19) of staff employees felt their contributions to Cooperative Extension are appreciated by management. One staff employee who agreed wrote, "Especially by my superior." Eighteen percent (5) of staff employees had no knowledge and 14% (4) disagreed that they felt their contributions to Cooperative Extension are appreciated by management. One staff employee who had no knowledge wrote, "Very loosely organized, not much feedback." All 3 (100%) of management felt the employees' contribution to Cooperative Extension are appreciated by management (see Table 4.37).

The subjects were asked one additional question directed specifically to them that was not closed end and asked to share any additional comments they would like to add.

Table 4.35

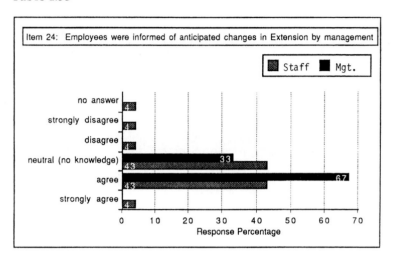

Item 24: Employees were informed of anticipated changes in Extension by management

Staff Employees

Question: How has management helped you to reach your performance objectives in face of downsizing?

#1   Our performance is up to the individual. They provide
     salary and some grant opportunities, that is all.
#3   (I) Have worked to maintain positive support by working
     for new funds. (The) Program I'm assigned to is already very
     small.
#9   Any downsizing has not directly affected me or my job.
#10 Downsizing in California CE was by attrition & retirement,
     not by firing. Those who remain fill in the gaps as best they
     can. The rest of the work does not get done.
#11 There has been no downsizing since I was employed.
#14 Allowing (me) a sabbatical leave.
#15 (I) Didn't know we were downsizing.
#16 Downsizing is not something I was aware of.
#18 Downsizing has forced us to prioritize and quit doing some
     of the ridiculous things we've been doing for years, such as
     4-H clubs.
#20 Being supportive of my work and being treated as a person
     of importance.

Table 4.36

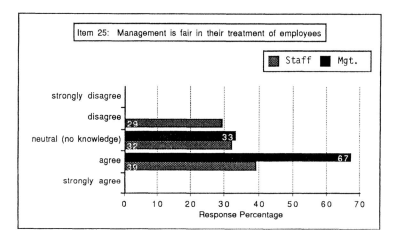

#22   No help at all. You are expected to be innovative. You are the leader. They are just managers.

#25   Provided desktop computer - First in (my) career that I didn't raise own funds to purchase.

#26   Through program and financial support. The understanding of program problems has helped. Good computer, printer, software, and copier.

Table 4.37

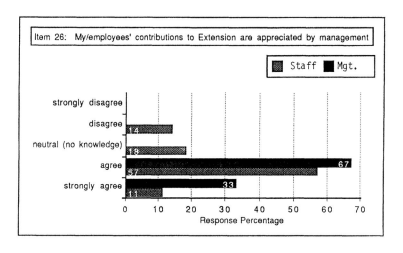

#27   Giving flexibility to complete assignments.

#28   We aren't downsizing (to the best of my knowledge).

Additional comments:

  #6   I am a new part time employee. I don't have much knowl-
        edge about how UCCE (University of California Coopera-
        tive Extension) operates at this time.

#12   We are faced with reduction in resources, but to date we
        have not released staff.

#14   The biggest problem in Extension is the lack of clear vision and
        direction. If there is clear vision, it is not being communicated
        to staff. Also, the organization also lacks inspired leadership.
        What leadership there is is generally directed at other organi-
        zations - not to work staff. Also, rewards (financial) are VERY
        slow rather than direct in terms of behavior reinforcement.

#20   These questions do not really look at technology advances
        within our offices. Some offices have too much. Some have
        not enough. Some offices have a few computers and others
        have individual computers.

#22   We are expected to do more with less resources but at the
        same time we are expected to work only 8-5 (pm) 100%.

#23   All of the downsizing has been done so far without layoffs
        which greatly impact morale.

#25   Management at all levels keeps expecting more & more after
        downsizing & budget reductions. Say they are supportive of
        employees who stop taking on more duties, but they keep
        heaping on more demands.

Management

What are you doing to maintain the mission of Cooperative Extension after Staff reduction?

  #1   Encourage staff to collaborate, internally and externally.
        Encourage and support staff to seek external funding.

  #3   Treading water!

Additional comments:

  #1   As County Director, I *am* "management" at the local level -
        My comments regarding management reflect the state and
        regional administration.

Illinois

Item 1: An ideal work environment should include the following:

Eighty-nine percent (17) of staff employees selected flexible scheduling, 83% (15) friendly co-worker, 77% (14) input on assignments, 61% (11) personal computer, and 50% (9) other as their choices of an ideal work environment. They listed under other the following: team work, non-threatening environment, trust, knowing there is a fair supervisor available for consultation if needed, pleasant environment, lights and plants, team players, team work, stability of job and (an) administrator who can actually administer continuous feedback, two way communication, trust and respect, and people who support the program. Nine (100%) of management selected friendly co-workers office space, 8 (89%) flexible scheduling and input on assignment, and 2 (22%) other as their choices of an ideal work environment (see Table 4.38). For the category other, management listed: recognition and human and financial resources.

Item 2: An ideal method for communicating anticipated downsizing to employees is:

Eighty-three percent (15) of staff employees selected employee meetings as their choice for an ideal method for communicating

Table 4.38

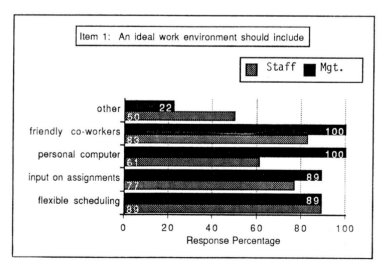

anticipated downsizing to them. Eleven percent (11) of them listed other and 6% (1) office memos. The other choices they wrote included: face to face meetings with superior and personal meetings. Nine (100%) of management selected employee meetings and 1 (11%) other as their choices for an ideal method of communicating anticipated downsizing to employees (see Table 4.39). The choice listed as other by management was personal contact.

Item 3: The following number of employees working in county offices have been promoted in the last 5 years:

Fifty-five percent (10) of the staff employees did not know how many employees working in county offices have been promoted in the last 5 years. One of these employees wrote, "Not sure (about the) exact count except in our county." Twenty-eight percent (5) of staff employees selected 1–3 employees promoted and 17% (3) selected 10 or more employees promoted in the last 5 years. Five (56%) of management selected 1–3 employees promoted, 1 (11%) selected 3–6 promoted, and 2 (22%) chose 10 or more employees promoted in the last 5 years. One (11%) of management did not answer this item (see Table 4.40).

Item 4: The following number of employees working in county offices have been promoted in the last 10 years.

Table 4.39

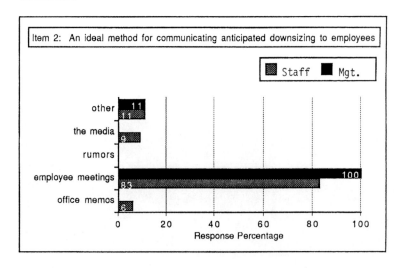

Table 4.40

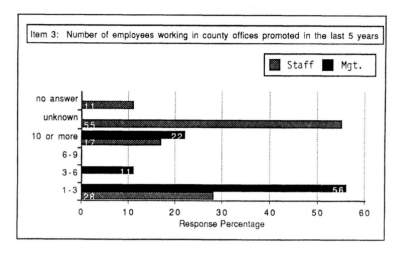

Seventy-two percent (13) of staff employees did not know the number of employees working in county offices that have been promoted in the last 10 years. However, one did write, "Have not worked here long enough, but 10 or more." Seventeen percent (3) of the staff employees selected 10 or more, five and one half percent (1) 1–3 and five and one half percent (1) 3–6 as the number of employees promoted in the last 10 years in county offices. Six (67%) of management selected 1–3 employees promoted in the last 10 years and one (11%) selected 3–6 and 10 or more employees promoted in the last 10 years. One (11%) of management did not answer this item (see 4.41).

Item 5: My general response or employees general response to an unfavorable performance evaluation is to:

Sixty-one percent (11) of staff employees selected ask for assistance as their general response to an unfavorable performance evaluation. Forty-four percent (8) of staff employees selected work harder, 6% (1) do nothing, and 11% (2) other. The choices written under the other category are: make sure I know where I need to work harder and those areas, never had an unfavorable performance, don't know, never had one, and ask for specific ways to improve from your supervisor. Five (56%) of management felt employees generally do nothing in response to an unfavorable

Table 4.41

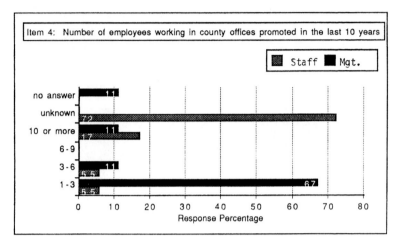

performance evaluation. Four (44%) of management selected ask for assistance; 2 (22%) selected work harder and sabotage the company in some way for the way they felt employees would react in response to an unfavorable performance evaluation (see Table 4.42).

Item 6: My general response or employees general response to a positive performance evaluation is to:

Table 4.42

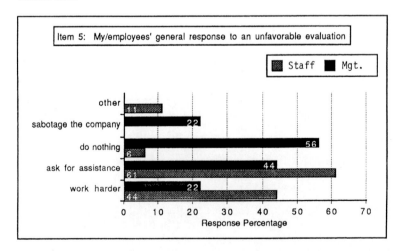

Sixty-seven percent (12) of staff employees selected work harder as their response to a positive performance evaluation. Thirty-three percent (6) of staff employees selected work satisfactorily and expected advancement as their response to a positive performance evaluation. Seventeen percent (3) of staff employees selected other. Their choices for other included: ask administrator where he thinks I can improve, salary increase, and continue to meet challenges. Five (56%) of management selected work satisfactorily as employees general response to a positive performance evaluation. Four (44%) of management felt employees work harder after a positive performance evaluation. Two (11%) of management felt employees would expect advancement after a positive performance evaluation (see Table 4.43).

Item 7: I first heard or employees were first notified about Cooperative Extension's plan to downsize by:

Eighty-three percent (15) of staff employees felt they heard about Cooperative Extension's plan to downsize through rumors. Twenty-two percent (4) of staff employees selected employee meeting; 17% (3) selected other; and 11% (2) selected the media as the way they heard about Cooperative Extension's plan to downsize. The other way staff employees responses listed under other are: didn't know about it on the national level, mail, and e-mail. Four (44%) of management felt employees were first notified about

Table 4.43

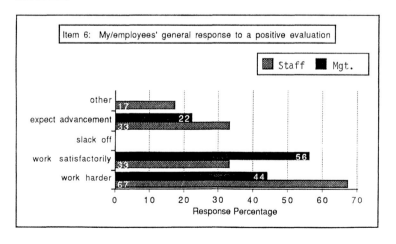

Cooperative Extension's plan to downsized by rumors. Three (33%) of management selected employee meeting, 2 (22%) the media, and 1 (11%) office memos as the way they thought employees were first notified about Cooperative Extension's plan to downsize (see Table 4.44).

Item 8: Rank the following incentives in order of importance to employees with 5 being extremely important and 1 being least important.

When ask to rank employee incentives in the order of importance with 5 being extremely important and 1 being least important, staff employees and management ranked *merit increase* the highest at 3. 78 and 4.22 respectively. Staff employees ranked *promotion opportunities* at 3.4, *other* at 3.0, *empowerment* at 2.9, and 2.7 for *bonus.* They listed the following choices under *other:* appreciation, some kind of recognition, employment security, and salary increase. Management ranked *empowerment* at 3.11, *promotion opportunities* at 2.78, *bonus* at 2.0, and 1.0 for *other* (see Table 4.45). Respect was listed under *other* for management.

The responses to Part II were:

1.   Strongly Agree
2.   Agree

Table 4.44

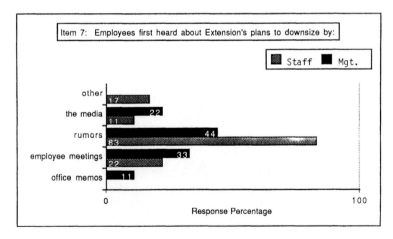

Table 4.45

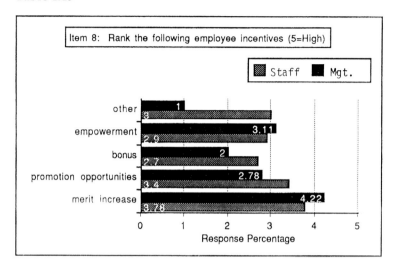

3. Neutral (No Knowledge)
4. Disagree
5. Strongly Disagree

Item 9: Employees are able to advance within the Cooperative Extension System.

Sixty-one percent (11) of staff employees felt that employees could advance within the Cooperative Extension and fifty-six percent (5) of management felt it was possible. Thirty-nine percent (7) of staff employees disagreed that employees are able to advance within Cooperative Extension. Thirty-three percent (3) of management felt employees were not able to advance within the Cooperative Extension System. Eleven percent (1) of management had no knowledge of whether employees could advance in Cooperative Extension (see Table 4.46).

Item 10: Management is consistent in their treatment of employees or all employees are treated consistently by management.

The majority of staff employees, 83% (15) and 8 (89%) of management felt management is not consistent in their treatment of employees. However, 17% (3) of staff employees and one (11%) of management had no knowledge of whether management is

Table 4.46

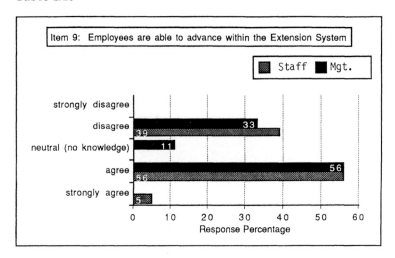

consistent in their treatment of employees (see Table 4.47). One of the staff employee wrote, "(It) depends on (the) administrator."
Item 11: Release time is allowed for staff to attend professional/skill development workshops.

Eighty-eight percent (16) of staff employees and 9 (100%) of management felt that release time is allowed for staff to attend workshops for professional and skill development. Six percent (1) of staff disagreed or had no knowledge whether release time was allowed for staff to attend professional/skill development workshops (see Table 4.48).

Item 12: I received or all employees are given a clearly written job description upon employment by Cooperative Extension.

Seventy-two percent (13) of staff employees felt they received a clearly written job description when they were employed by Cooperative Extension. Five (56%) of management felt employees received a clearly written job description when they were employed. Seventeen percent (3) of staff employees disagreed and 11% (2) felt they had no knowledge of whether employees got a clearly written job description when they were employed. Three (33%) of management also disagreed that employees received a

Table 4.47

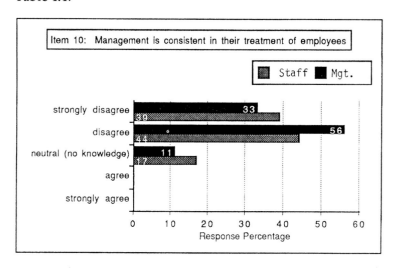

Item 10:   Management is consistent in their treatment of employees

Staff   Mgt.

Table 4.48

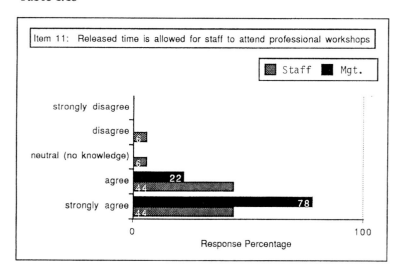

Item 11:   Released time is allowed for staff to attend professional workshops

Staff   Mgt.

clearly written job description when they were employed by Cooperative Extension. One (11%) management had no knowledge of whether employees received a clearly written job description when they were hired (see Table 4.49).

Item 13: The program budget allows for employees to attend training workshops.

Sixty-one percent (11) of staff employees and six (67%) of management felt the program budget allows for employees to attend training workshops. Thirty-nine percent (7) of staff employees and 3 (33%) of management disagreed that the program budget allows for employees to attend training workshops (see Table 4.50). One staff employee that disagreed wrote, "Mine does, other don't".

Item 14: Employees are given a verbal warning about unsatisfactory performance before receiving an unfavorable job evaluation.

Fifty percent (9) of staff employees did not agree that employees are given a verbal warning about unsatisfactory performance before receiving an unfavorable job evaluation. Only 4 (44%) of management was in disagreement. Two (22%) of management felt employees are given a verbal warning before receiving an unfavorable job evaluation. Three (33%) of management and 39% (7) of staff employees had no knowledge. Five and one half percent (1) of staff employees felt employees are given a verbal warning before receiving an unfavorable job evaluation. Five and one half percent (1) of staff employees did not answer this item (see Table 4.51).

Table 4.49

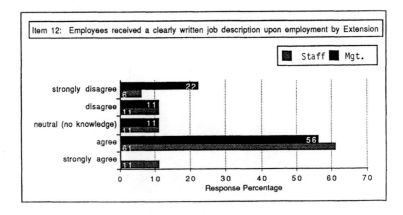

Item 12: Employees received a clearly written job description upon employment by Extension

Staff ■ Mgt.

strongly disagree	22 / 6
disagree	11 / 11
neutral (no knowledge)	11 / 11
agree	56 / 61
strongly agree	11

Response Percentage

Table 4.50

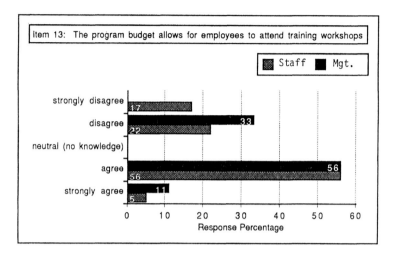

Item 15: Training is provided by management to assist employees in performing their job.

Forty-four percent (8) of staff employees and 5 (56%) of management felt training is provided by management to assist employees in performing their job. Thirty-nine percent (7) of staff

Table 4.51

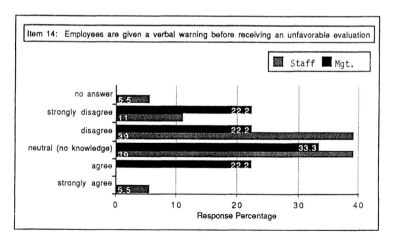

employees and 4 (44%) management felt management did not provide training to assist employees in performing their job. Seventeen percent (3) of staff employee felt that they had no knowledge of whether management provided training to assist employees (see Table 4.52).

Item 16: Employee incentives encourage increased output.

Forty-four percent (8) of staff employees and only 2 (22%) of management felt employee incentives encourage increased output. Forty-four percent (8) of staff employees disagreed that employee incentives encourages increased output. However, the majority of management, 6 (67%) disagreed that employee incentives encourage increased output. Both 11% (2) of staff employees and 1 (11%) of management felt they had no knowledge whether employee incentives encourages increased output (see Table 4.53).

Item 17: Employees are able to perform at the same level as they did before Cooperative Extension downsized their county offices.

The majority 83% (15) of staff employee and 8 (88%) of management did not think employees could perform at the same level as they did before Cooperative Extension downsized. Eleven percent (2) of staff employees felt employees are able to perform at the same level as they did before downsizing. Six percent (1) of staff employees did not answer this item and wrote, "(It was a) poor

Table 4.52

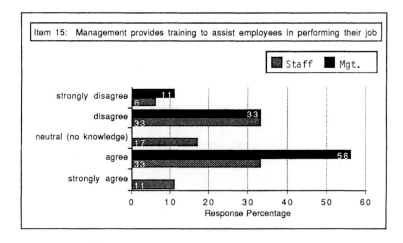

Table 4.53

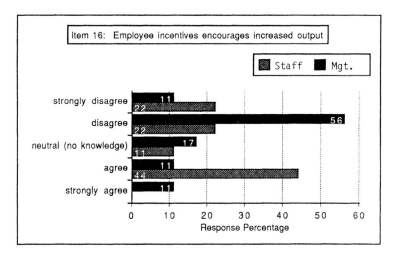

question". One (11%) of management felt they had no knowledge of whether employees are able to perform at the same level as they did before downsizing (see Table 4.54).

Item 18: The employees' performance level decreased after Cooperative Extension downsized their county offices.

Table 4.54

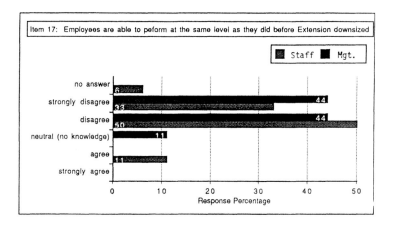

Thirty-nine percent (7) of staff employees and 6 (67%) of management felt employees' level of performance decreased after Cooperative Extension downsized their county offices. Thirty-three and one half percent (6) of staff employees disagreed that employees' level of performance decreased after downsizing. Five and one half percent (1) of staff employees did not answer this item. Eleven percent (1) of staff employees and 1 (11%) of management had no knowledge of whether employees' level of performance decreased after Cooperative Extension downsized their county offices (see Table 4.55).

Item 19: Support or assistance provided by management to perform my duties decreased after Cooperative Extension downsized their county offices.

Sixty-one percent (11) of staff employees and 7 (78%) of management agreed that support or assistance by management decreased after Cooperative Extension downsized their county offices. Twelve percent (2) of staff employees did not think that support or assistance by management decreased after downsizing. Twenty-two percent (4) of staff employees had no knowledge of whether support or assistance by management decreased after downsizing. Five percent (1) of staff did not answer this item. One

Table 4.55

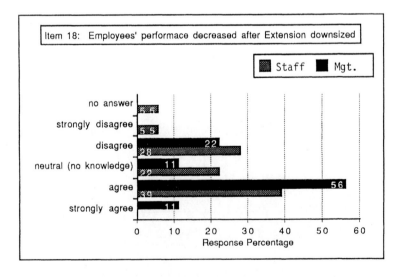

(11%) of management disagreed or had no knowledge of whether support or assistance by management decreased after Cooperative Extension downsized their county offices (see Table 4.56). One of management wrote, "I never experienced support from Day One! I have been recognized for many outstanding programs, but have no idea how my director feels."

Item 20: The technology provided by Cooperative Extension improved my or employees' job performance.

Fifty percent (9) of staff employees and only 22% (2) of management felt the technology provided by Cooperative Extension improved employees' job performance. The majority of management, 7 (78%) disagreed that the technology provided by Cooperative Extension improved employees' job performance. One of management who disagreed wrote, "CES (Cooperative Extension System) has not provided." Thirty-three percent (6) of staff employees disagreed and 3 (17%) had no knowledge of whether technology provided by Cooperative Extension improved employees' job performance (see Table 4.57).

Item 21: Management provided timely and accurate information about their downsizing.

The majority, 89% (16) of staff employee and 66% (6) of management did not think that management provided timely and accurate information about their downsizing. A very small number of

Table 4.56

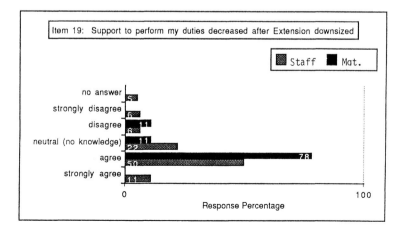

Table 4.57

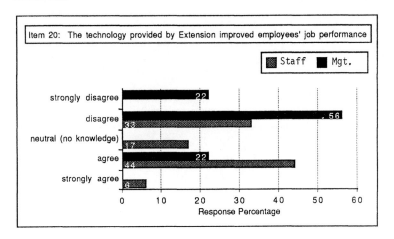

management, 1 (11%) and 5.5% (1) of staff employees felt timely and accurate information was provided by management. Five and one half percent (1) of staff employee and 2 (22%) of management had no knowledge of whether management provided timely and accurate information about downsizing (see Table 4.58).

Item 22: I am responsible or employees are responsible only for duties listed on the written job description.

The majority, 83% (15) of staff employees and 8 (89%) of management felt employees are responsible for more duties than those listed on their written job description. However, 17% (3) of staff employees agreed that they are responsible for only duties listed on their written job description. Two people who disagreed wrote that, "It's very vague and new assignments are continuously appearing". One (11%) of management had no knowledge of whether employees are responsible for only duties listed on their written job description (see Table 4.59).

Item 23: Trust can be rebuilt in organizations faced with downsizing.

Sixty-one percent (11) of staff employees and 6 (67%) of management felt trust can be rebuilt in organizations faced with downsizing. Twenty-two percent (4) of staff employees and 2 (22%) of management disagreed that trust can be rebuilt in organizations faced with downsizing. One staff employee who disagreed wrote,

Table 4.58

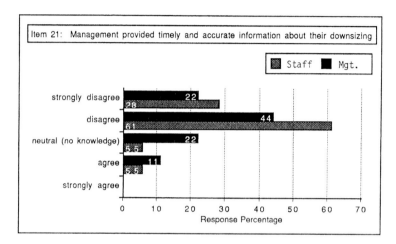

Table 4.59

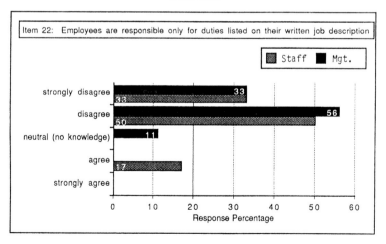

Table 4.59

"Depends on how it is done." One of management who had no knowledge of whether trust can be rebuilt after downsizing wrote, "If the administration continue to do what the(y) have always done-NO-trust can be rebuilt." Seventeen percent (3) of staff employees and 1 (11%) percent of management had no knowledge of whether trust can be rebuilt in organizations faced with downsizing (see Table 4.60).

Item 24: Employees were informed of anticipated changes in Cooperative Extension by management before downsizing.

Thirty-nine percent (7) of staff employees and 3 (33%) of management agreed employees were informed of anticipated changes in Cooperative Extension by management before downsizing. One staff employee who agreed wrote, "Downsizing was handled by retirement incentives." Seventeen percent (3) of staff employees and 1 (11%) of management had no knowledge about whether employees were informed of anticipated changes in Cooperative Extension by management before downsizing. Forty-three percent (8) of staff employees and 5 (56%) of management disagreed that employees were informed of anticipated changes in Cooperative Extension by management before downsizing (see Table 4.61).

Item 25: Management is fair in their treatment of employees.

Table 4.60

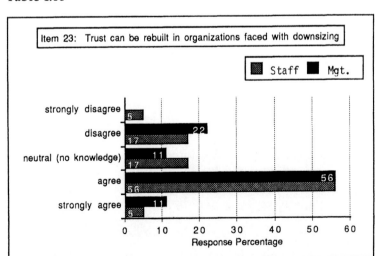

Table 4.61

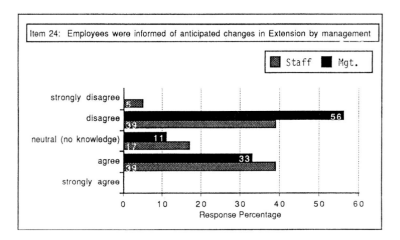

Item 24: Employees were informed of anticipated changes in Extension by management

Staff   Mgt.

Most of staff employees, 67% (12) and 5 (55%) of management did not feel that management is fair in their treatment of employees. One of the staff employee who disagreed that management is fair in their treatment of employees wrote, "This is only for the rumor mill." Eleven percent (2) of staff employees and 3 (33%) of management felt management is fair in their treatment of employees. Twenty-two percent (4) of staff employees and 1 (11%) of management had no knowledge of whether management is fair in their treatment of employees (see Table 4.62).

Item 26: My contributions or employees'contributions to Cooperative Extension are appreciated by management.

Fifty-five percent (10) of staff employees and 4 (44%) of management felt employees' contribution to Cooperative Extension are appreciated by management. Thirty-three percent (6) of staff employees and 2 (22%) of management did not think the employees' contribution to Cooperative Extension are appreciated by management. Eleven percent (2) of staff employees and 3 (33%) of management had no knowledge of whether employees' contributions to Cooperative Extension are appreciated by management (see Table 4.63).

The subjects were asked one additional question directed specifically to them that was not closed end and asked to share any additional comments they would like to add.

Table 4.62

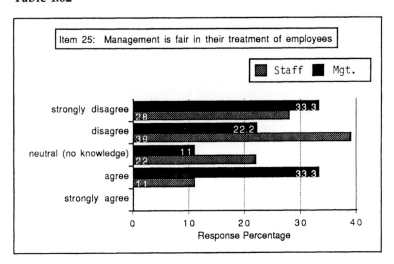

Table 4.63

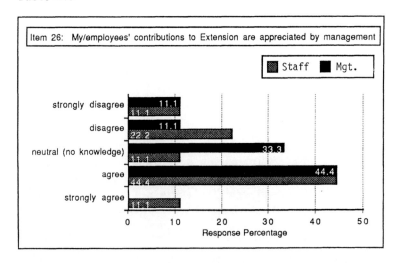

Staff Employees

Question: How has management helped you to reach your performance objective in face of downsizing?

  #2   Appear to be too busy with other tasks to offer much assistance to those that apparently can get along without assistance.
  #3   Very little, not much contact with (my) supervisor.
  #6   No, I meet them on my own despite downsizing.
  #7   I have not been directly affected by the downsizing, but my Regional Director was exceptional in explaining my role upon being hired.
 #10   No assistance.
 #11   They have not.
 #13   Initially - more inservice - then there was a drastic decrease. More technology that was current 6 years ago, but (is) now out of date.
 #15   Hasn't occurred - more work given with more counties to cover with same clientele expectations as before downsizing. Even administration is downsized so (there is) no one in management to assist you.
 #16   They haven't. I try to keep as many programs going as possible.

Additional comments:

  #5   Employees need to be informed and treated equally.
  #7   I was not employed with Extension during the downsizing in '91, so I did not know exactly how management handled the situation.
        I do know about some of the closing of centers.
 #13   We have been downsized numerous times. The (19) 91 was the worse and the process was the most - *poorly handled.*
(The) Worse morale occurred at that time and most "old timers" no longer trust (the) system.
 #15   Downsizing occurred from (the) top down with decisions made from (the) top down. No employee input (was) ask(ed) for.
 #18   The secretaries, in many cases, because of years of service and the non move forward viewpoint, have made all changes

harder for the public to accept. Making it harder for the rest of us to move forward. Management were not open about any points of downsizing. The media released it before counties and centers even knew about it.

Management

What are you doing to maintain the mission of Cooperative Extension after staff reduction?

#1 Employees are asked to do more.
#3 Increase local support and do the best I can.
#4 We had no staff reduction in our office. We have been more creative in programming with less professional staff available.
#7 I am working twice as hard and saying "NO" - We don't do that any longer more often.
I wish to hire non-academic help to pick up the load and the administration. A volunteer could do. County councils want ownership, especially if they are funding the office and staff.

Additional comments:

#2 Management does not have a good procedure to determine effectiveness of staff. (They) Rely on written reports which may, and usually does not, identify most effective employees.
#7 With the ICES (Illinois Cooperative Extension System) downsizing and revitalization, administration/Regional Directors are not accepting the fact that the action/happening are from the bottom up. We must be:

Customer focused, inspiring/pursuing high goals, strive for continuous improvement, develop a stronger and more positive reputation. Act with customer bias and seek further funding. The 100 year old paradigms don't work today. We also need to get away from the administrative arrogance and accept/listen to staff who are working in the trenches with citizens.

THE INTERVIEW

For the interview process, a set of questions was used to elicit information regarding the perceptions of the participants and to provide additional data for the study. Interviews were conducted over the phone. Participants who indicated in the initial consent agreement (see Appendix F) that they would participate in the interview process were contacted to find out if they were still interested.

Ten participants from California and ten from Illinois were interviewed at their convenience. The interviews were conducted over a three week time frame because some participants were out of the office. Three interviews had to be conducted later due to the participant's schedule.

Question 1. Were you aware that Cooperative Extension is/ was in the process of downsizing?

  a. How did this information affect you?
  b. Did this information affect your job outcome?
  (#19) Yes
      a. It didn't. Our office is small. There were some budget cuts, but it didn't affect my salary or anything.
      b. No
  (#10) Oh, yes!
      a. It has really affected me. It has been unfortunate to the organization. There are more problems, but less people to deal with them. Some of the critical problems are not addressed. There is more work than I can take on, speaking in terms of Agriculture and not Home Economics or Youth programs. There are a lot of agencies that come to Extension to have products tested. The University provides unbiased information to them, which is something they need. They still want the University's "Stamp of Approval."
      b. (I) can't address all the critical problems.
  (#31) Oh, yeah!
      a. In California, our downsizing created more work, but it didn't change my security.
      b. It determined what was going to get done and what was not.
  (#8) Ah, yes.
      a. Ah, In what way? I guess the work environment may be a little more stressful.
      b. No, as far as I know.
  (#26) I didn't think so, but now I know it is.
      a. It has not.

b. It did in the sense of being able to coordinate with other people.

(#13) Yes

a. Very strongly. The state of California is divided into regions. In my region, North Central, the County Directors and Regional Director got together and decided which areas (programs) were more important than others. They decided that my position (Public Issues Education) was low priority.

b. My position got low priority. They wanted to cut my position, but I negotiated for another year so that I could retire in April. So, I was more or less forced to retire. There is a move in California back to commodities. Programs, such as consumer sciences and youth programs are not getting the priorities like agriculture.

(#30) Yes

a. I lost staff members.

b. No

(#27) Yes

a. It didn't, not personally.

b. No

(#12) Yes

a. We have taken on a greater work load because there are fewer persons to do it.

b. Not me personally.

(#28) No

a. It didn't.

b. No

In Illinois, the majority of the respondents were aware that Cooperative Extension had downsized. Two of them stated that was how they had gotten their jobs. They responded:

(#5) Yes

a. Well, I came in as an hourly academic after my position was vacated through retirement. Then the position was frozen. I don't have a master's degree, so nothing was available to me. I was in limbo for three (3) years as an hourly academic. I was an interim employee and was not able to advance.

(#10) Yes

    a. Actually that's how I got my job. The person that had the job before me was downsized out. We got some local funding and I got the job.

    b. Yes, I don't know if I (will) have a job from year to year.

Others replied:

(#12) Yeah

    a. Illinois has been downsizing for the last ten (10) years. When I was hired, they informed me about the downsizing, the organizational changes and how my job would fit into the scheme.

    b. No, it hasn't. Well, it has to some degree. The resources are less. We have limited programs and are looking at new ways of initiating things (programs) because we don't have the staff.

(#20) Yes

    a. Ah, I work in Extension Services

    b. No

(#19) Yes, I just came back from a North Central Regional meeting where many of the states are going through the same type of downsizing or reorganization. In Illinois, 1991 we had a reorganization and lose a lot of employees, but a year later we have about the same number that we lose.

    a. When we first heard about it, we didn't know how it would affect us. We were a little apprehensive. A lot was unknown, so we felt some anxiety.

    b. Not really, my title changed, but I was able to stay in the county. Our jobs are locally funded and I think they have money for us.

(#25) Yes

    a. It affected us in that educators are based in the field. When downsizing occurred, we were not able to address as many problems or the problems in a timely manner.

    b. Well, it does in a sense in that if clientele wanted to have a program in a certain time frame, we were not able to meet the needs.

(#22) Yeah

    a. It didn't affect me personally.

    b. Yes, we lose resources.
(#20) Very aware
    a. We went from ten (10) people with my job title to five
    (5). It expanded my territory substantially.
    b. My position got watered down, so we are not as effec-
    tive as we were.
(#24) Sure
    a. Not at all.
    b. No, not really.
(#13) Yes
    a. I was not happy.
    b. Just slightly, we only lost one person. It wasn't as hard
    to pick up his work load as it was with other teams that
    lost half of their staff. Since then we lost more because
    they quit. We have more work load.

Question 2. Do you feel secure in your job? If not, why?

(#19) Yes, very much so. I have a very understanding boss.
(#13) I am secure for another year, but I would have liked to
work longer.
(#30) Pretty secure.

Those in Illinois who felt secure in their job stated:

(#12) Yeah, my job is county funded. We get a six (6) months
notice before termination and after three (3) years employment,
a year notice. I think that wouldn't be any different than any
other job I might have.
(#5) Ah, as much as the 90's allow. If funds are available, the
position will be there. In the 70's and 80's, jobs were more secure.
I have to be realistic.
(#22) Yes, I would say so. We are locally funded.

Those who did not feel secure in California stated:

(#27) No, even though I've been on the job, my job depends on
the budget. The budget changes from one year to the next.
(#12) Compared to twenty years ago, when I first started working, I feel less secure but I am not worried that next year I would
not have a job.

We have to be a little more creative in getting funds. In Illinois, they said, "No, even though I am funded for another year, My job depends on funding from the city (#10); No, I have a year to year assignment. I had tenure when I taught school (#25); and Not really, there is no real security anymore. We had ten (10) Regional Directors and now we have five (5). I went from county to region. In 1991 everybody was fired. We had to reapply and be interviewed for the positions that were available. One third of the Extension staff was lost. We had one hundred fifty (150) positions in 1991. As of now, we only have one hundred (100) position. In five (5) years, we have one third less staff. We had fifty (50) State Specialist. We are down to nine (9) full time (equivalent) and three (3) part-time Specialist (#13)."

Question 3. Do you believe Cooperative Extension provides upward mobility to its employees?

   a. Are you interested in advancing within the university system?
   b. Have you had an opportunity to advance within the university system?
   c. How does Cooperative Extension assist or prepare its employees for advancement?

(#19) Yes, depending on your program. I think there are opportunities for growth.

   a. Yes
   b. No
   c. They provide lots of opportunities. My supervisor encourages me to do things to improve my skills and prepare me for advancement. I attend classes.

(#10) Yes, if you do your job.

   a. Yes, I'm, working on the next notch.
   b. Yes, I have been with Extension all my life, (that is) my professional life. I have been with UC for eighteen years and have advanced several steps.
   c. There have been some workshops that help people to get on track, prepare a dolce (vita), and attract people who you will be working with. Young people may be led astray, generally speaking, but after the workshop, I call them to set the record straight.

(#31) Oh, yeah.
    a. Yeah, but with downsizing there might not be as much opportunity to.
    b. Oh, yeah.
    c. In the UC system, not very well. Any training that is needed, you'd have to figure out for yourself. Most of the promotions are from within. They give you the keys to building and say, "You figure it out." Make it work.

(#8) Yes
    a. Yes
    b. Yes
    c. Well, it totally depends on the mentoring relationship with the County Director. I have a good relationship with my County Director. I would say guidance from administration.

(#26) Not much.
    a. Not really. I see my future in another field - environmental education.
    b. No
    c. They partially prepare employees for advancement.

(#13) Generally, yes.
    a. Not really. If you happen to be in a program that attracts the most money to the University, you'd probably advance. There's a lot of emphasis on getting a Ph. D., writing journal articles, and doing research. Just doing your program does not advance you.
    b. Yes, I moved from a staff employee to County Director and to an Advisor.
    c. I don't know if they really do. Maybe tuition reimbursement.

(#30) Yes
    a. No
    b. No
    c. Well, advancement is within the academic rank. There is a lot of consultation between your peers and academia.

(#27) No
    a. Not personally. You can't advance without a college degree and I don't have one.
    c. It doesn't. If they assist employees, they would provide a list of how to get to the next step. I think they do

provide a percentage of tuition if the schooling is job related and approved by the supervisor.

(#12) I personally wouldn't want to change. The salary scale in California is wonderful. As the Home Economist, I wouldn't want to change to upper level positions, like administration.

    a. See above.

    b. I am not interested in advancement.

    c. We have training funds provided to each advisor for professional development, as long as it is within the job requirements.

(#28) Um, across the board, I would say no.

    a. Yes

    b. No

    c. Um, through scholarship monies for continuing education. But it has to be within the department's budget. Fifty percent has to be matched by (the) program budget, so you may get approved, but there is no money. I was approved for a scholarship, but the department didn't have the funds.

The Illinois respondents replied saying:

(#12) To some degree. They provide education, but the positions are limited. The classes are free for employees at the University of Illinois.

    a. Not necessarily in this system, but maybe in another state after I complete my education.

    b. It depends on your education. However, this is the first year they integrated promotions. I had an opportunity to apply. They do it for the Masters' level, but they expanded it (promotions) for Bachelors' level. You can get to the second level, but you need a Master degree for the third level. You have six (6) years to attain a Master.

(#5) No. I think there is a move toward that direction. I have been here eight (8) years. Five of those years as a unit assistant. I received modest raises and was at the same status. The Regional Director is indicating I (should) get a Master's degree. I don't see any incentive even though money is an incentive, but for eight hundred (800) additional dollars, it is not worth it for me. I work fifty (50) plus hours per week and my schedule just doesn't allow for school. I would need release time which is somewhat negotiable.

    a. No, I would have to relocate and it wouldn't be beneficial for my family.

    b. No

    c. They provide a ranking system for Extension Educators and Unit Leaders, but this system is not open for Unit Assistants.

(#10) It depends on what you want in upward mobility. Yes, in Illinois you stay at the education level and move to the second and third level. It may be very little mobility in administration because of all the cuts.

    a. No, not to the administrative level.

    b. No

    c. I think they do very little.

(#20) No

    a. Yes

    b. That's hard to answer. I would say, "Yes" and "No," but probably *"No"*.

    c. They provide opportunities for continuing education.

(#19) I guess, I would have to say, "Yes" and "No." At the county level there is not a lot of room for advancement, but on the other hand, you can advance statewide.

    a. No

    b. Yeah, through the last ?? reorganization, I did. I could have gone elsewhere, to another locale, but I choose to stay in this county.

    c. In the old system, pre-91, we had mentors like the Home Economist and Farm Advisors, but in the new system there is no training in place. We are in the process of preparing job descriptions and an evaluation system.

(#25) I don't know.

    a. No, I am close to retirement.

    b. Yes

    c. Poorly, no preparation, I think.

(#22) Yes, it does.

    a. Probably not.

    b. No, I have only been with the University a few years.

    c. They provide opportunities, but it's up to the individual to pursue them.

(#24) No, not one hundred (100) percent.
   a. No
   b. Yes
   c. Ah, actually, they don't. They do require employees with a Bachelor degree to a Master.
(#10) I am not sure. There are less positions to apply for. We had five (5) ranks, now we have three (3).
   a. I'm not interested in an administrative position. I would consider a State Specialist position because, I like working with people. Administrators really don't get a chance to do that any more. But the State Specialist position requires a Ph. D., which I don't have.
   b. One time. I had an opportunity for position that was vacant, but the person who left it didn't like his new position and came back. We had five (5) ranks, now we have three (3).

Question 4. If upward mobility is possible, do you think downsizing will impact your changes for advancement?

(#10) Not sure. Don't know. We are peer reviewed. As you get to the the top of the system, you have very few peers. I know only one (1) person at Step 8. The review pool gets slim. I don't know what impact that has or whether people will help or not. If you've made enemies along the way, it may be difficult. In lower ranks, you probably would have enough people who could make a fair assessment.
(#30) I am not interested in advancement.
(#12) I haven't given this much thought, since I am not interested.

One respondent in Illinois who felt the same said, "I haven't thought about it. It is not an issue with me. But, I don't think the positions are there (#10)." Other comments in California were:

(#19) No, even though there were budget cuts, our office has remained the same.
(#31) It is hard to judge. I guess it depends on your goals and objectives. As a result of downsizing, the mechanism used and how you fit into what is needed may be different.
(#8)   No

(#26) Of course.

(#13) Yeah, I have to retire. I think people will hold their jobs longer. The possibility of paras (paraprofessionals) being Advisors probably won't happen. Lower rank Advisors will not move up. Years ago there were opportunities for Advisors to move into Specialist positions, but I see fewer of them becoming Specialists.

(#27) Yes

(#28) Sure

Two of the respondents in Illinois did not think that downsizing would impact their chances of advancement because, "Positions are based on county support (#5)" and the other respondent was close to retirement. He stated, "Well, not really, I'd like to clarify some of my answers. I have been with Extension for over thirty (30) years and I am close to retirement, so I am not thinking about advancement (#24).

The others who felt that downsizing impacts upward mobility said, "Yes (#20) and (#25); Sure (#20) and (#22); and Definitely (#13)." They responded:

(#12) Yeah, it has. It has eliminated a number of positions. I would be interested in.

(#19) Yeah, I would say with any type of downsizing, there would be fewer jobs to go to.

Question 5. How has Cooperative Extension helped you to reach your performance objectives since downsizing?

(#19) There's really no changes in our office. The classes I attend are paid for by the University. They offer classes to help me improve my skills.

(#12) They allow training. There has been some training on grant writing. We are doing more things on a regional basis, rather than county.

Several of Illinois respondents felt Cooperative Extension had helped them. They replied:

(#5)   we have a certain amount of latitude to pursue our goals and improve ourselves. They provide workshops and training.

They have a great deal of tolerance for training and professional development.

(#10) In one instance, they paid for a seminar I attended, but it was paid out of local funds and not state or regional dollars. If funds are not raised by the local government, we can't participate.

(#22) They provide us an opportunity for continuing education.

(#20) They have provided out-of-state travel money.

(#24) They have provided inservice - educational opportunities. They have provided opportunities for everybody to understand where they are and what is expected of them.

(#13) They encouraged us to get specialized training through other organizations or within Extension. They even encourage us to go to Europe to find out about their horticulture and paid one third of our expenses. I wouldn't have been able to go without it. Our evaluations are based on how we remain current. You can lose your job, if you don't stay current.

Some respondents did not think that Cooperative Extension did anything to help them reach their performance objectives. California's respondents stated:

(#26) They haven't been very effective.

(#27) They really haven't, but the county has provided resources similar to how it was before, receptionists, secretaries, and support dollars. There has been talk about getting more computers, computer work stations, and chairs which I know isn't coming from the University. At least, I don't think so.

(#30) It has not.

Illinois respondents said:

(#12) Each employee set his/her own goals. So you set them for something that can be obtained in a year. We program prioritize so needs can be taken care of.

(#20) Ah, they have not.

(#19) I guess in my particular position since it's new, I have kind of been on my own. In the new positions, people don't know what to expect.

Two other respondents in California said, "They encouraged me to retire because my position is being phased out (#13)" and "I would say it has been laisez-faire. I've been here for four (4) years. I started a new program and cover four (4) counties (#23).

Question 6. In what way can Cooperative Extension assist you in reaching your performance objective?

California respondents had some interesting responses.

(#19) Job posting announcement not just in California, but in Extension all over. Scholarship money for continuing (my) education (would be helpful).

(#12) The University has high expectations for research and publishing. Assistance in these areas (training) would be helpful.

(#30) Each office is so individualized. It would be nice if I had someone to help with report writing. I am going to be realistic, so I would say more computer technology service or assistance.

(#27) They can provide me with more time in the office to complete my paperwork. My time is split 75% time in the field and 25% in the office. So, I guess a better distribution of my time.

(#13) They can provide performance evaluation and merit increases, but since 90% of the budget is for salaries, there is not a lot of monies for programs. There is a 3.5 percent cut on each program's budget that has occurred for the last couple of years that we can write grants for. Downsizing has affected any long range goals, I think.

(#26) Actually, the most critical for me is the development of curriculum like Minnesota and Texas. I would like to be able to develop curriculum like we used to. We are more in the modality of putting together what has already been developed.

The responses in Illinois were:

(#12) Even though we get free classes, there are some expenses involved. If we got assistance on expenses, that would be nice. A lot more resources would also be helpful. Specialists were based in county clusters of eight (8), now they serve eighteen (18) counties.

(#5) They are on the brink of a lot of changes. They are drafting performance objectives and appraisals for advancement for Unit Assistants. Provide workshops and training.

(#10) One of the problems in Illinois is that we don't have clear objectives about what is expected. I am at level I and we do have objectives, but not a lot of support from administration. I think they could provide improved training for staff. They provide inservice for teaching and working with diverse audiences, but not in specific areas like I'm in (horticulture). I like to see more continuing education and better linkages with the college in speciality areas.

(#25) They can't, we have no advocates. Assistance and secretaries have support, but we can't. Unit Leaders are out there on their own.

(#22) Nothing really, I just need to set my priorities and take advantage of the opportunities available. I need more hours in the day.

(#20) Provide support-from my superiors and extra money for traveling.

(#24) I would say a continuation of number 5 (Staff inservice - educational opportunities).

(#13) We now have computer, they can upgrade computer technology-wise so we can do a better job. They encourage us to work on quality of excellence. They are helping us with technology - provide Distance Learning. I am covering thirty-nine (39) counties, working fifteen (15) hour days. More staff would help, even if they just fill the positions where people have just quit.

READING AND REFERENCES

Brockner, J., Glover, S., & Blonder, M. D. (1988). Predictors of survivors 'job involvement following layoffs: A field study. *Journal of Applied Psychology*, 73(3), 436–442.

CHAPTER 5

Summary, Conclusion, and Recommendations

This study of Cooperative Extension staff provided insight into their perceptions of workplace morale in light of downsizing. The researcher posits impending changes in the organization lead to mistrust and insecurity, as well as possible reduction in job performance. Several researchers stated that when organizations understand the human reactions to change, they can better prepare for future reductions with the least amount of distress for their employees (Maynard, 1996; Nelton, 1996; Winston James & Li-Ping Tang, 1996; and Neal, 1996). This study was undertaken for this reason.

This study was pursued because reports on the empirical investigation of the multiple causes, consequences and dynamics of downsizing is limited (Cameron, 1994), especially for Extension Services. Although the researcher has no intentions of designing a guide of "how to" downsize, the results can be used to develop leadership training programs in light of downsizing in Cooperative Extension.

Cooperative Extension provides a very important service to the community they serve. It is important for staff to have a good attitude toward their workplace and the service they provide. In the chaos of downsizing, security is lost, communication is lacking, and employees are no longer at peak performance. Management needs to look at how the work environment influences the services provided by staff and make adjustments where needed.

CONCLUSIONS

General Information on Work Environment

1. Both staff employees and management felt an ideal work environment should include: flexible scheduling, input on assignments, personal computers, and friendly co-workers.
2. Both staff employees and management felt the employee meetings is an ideal method for communicating anticipated downsizing to employees.
3. The majority of staff employees and management indicated that staff had been promoted in the last 5–10 years.
4. The majority of staff employees and fifty percent of management felt that when employees receive an unfavorable performance evaluation, they should ask for assistance. Management also indicated that employees should work harder if they get an unfavorable evaluation. The same number felt the employee might sabotage the company if they were given an unsatisfactory evaluation.
5. Staff employees indicated that the employees general response to a positive performance evaluation is to work harder. Management also thought employee should work harder, but also indicated that some work satisfactorily after receiving a positive evaluation.
6. Staff employees and management felt that the program budget does allow for employees to attend training workshops.

Workplace Morale

7. Half of management was not aware that employees first heard about Cooperative Extensions plans to downsize by rumors.

When asked whether downsizing impacted their job outcome. Subjects responded: "It has really affected me. It has been unfortunate to the organization. There are more problems, but less people to deal with them. Some of the critical problems are not addressed. There is more work than I can take on . . . "(#10). In California, our downsizing created more work, but it didn't change my security" (#31). I would say very strongly. The state of California is divided into regions. In my region, North Central, the County Directors and Regional Director got together and decided which areas (programs) were more important than others. They decided that my position (Public Issues Education) was low priority" (#13).

8. Merit increase, promotion opportunities, and following closely behind was empowerment as important employee incentives to both staff employees and management.
9. The majority of staff employees and management felt that employees are able to advance in Cooperative Extension. However, since downsizing, there are not as many positions within their geographic location as there were years ago. Most of the participants interviewed stated that Cooperative Extension does provide opportunities for advancement. They commented, "Yes, if you do your job" (#10). Yeah, but with downsizing there might not be as much opportunity (#31).
10. Staff employees and management did not think that management is consistent in their treatment of employees.
11. Staff employees and management felt that released time is allowed for staff to attend professional/skill development workshops.
12. Both staff employees and management indicated that employees received clearly written job descriptions when they are hired by Extension.
13. The majority of management and some of staff employees indicated that support to perform their duties decreased after downsizing. However, several of the staff employees indicated that they had no knowledge of whether support decreased after downsizing.

Survivor Job Security

14. Staff employees and management felt that management does provide training to assist employees in performing their job. An Illinois interviewee commented, "We have a certain amount of latitude to pursue our goals and improve ourselves. They provide workshops and training. They have a great deal of tolerance for training and professional development" (#5). Another one said, "They have provided inservice

- educational opportunities. They have provided opportunities for everybody to understand where they are and what is expected of them" (#24). In California a comment was: "They allow training. There has been some training on grant writing. We are doing more things on a regional basis, rather than county" (#12).

15. A large proportion of staff employees felt that employee incentives encourage increased output, but management did not think it did.

16. Both staff employees and management felt that downsizing affected employees performance level. They indicated that employees' performance level decreased after Cooperative Extension downsized their county offices.

17. Staff employees felt that the technology provided by Cooperative Extension improved their job performance, but management did not think it did.

Trust (in the workplace)

18. Staff employees were divided on whether they thought employees are given a verbal warning about an unsatisfactory performance before receiving an unfavorable evaluation. However, management felt that employees do receive a warning first.

19. Staff employees and management felt that the staff was not given accurate and timely information regarding the downsizing.

20. Staff employees and management felt that employees are responsible for more duties than those listed on their written job description.

21. Staff employees and management felt that trust can be rebuilt in organizations faced with downsizing.

22. Most of the staff employees felt that they were informed of anticipated changes in Cooperative Extension by management. Management was equally divided on whether they felt management informed employees of anticipated changes in Cooperative Extension.

23. Many of the staff employees felt that management was not fair in their treatment of employees. However, several of them thought that they were fair in their treatment of employees.

Management was equally divided on whether they felt management was fair in their treatment of employees.

24. The majority of staff employees and management felt that employees' contributions to Cooperative Extension are appreciated by management.

RECOMMENDATIONS

Based on the preceding conclusions, the following recommendations are offered:

1. Develop a system to improve communication between employees and management.
2. Provide continuous feedback to employees regarding future downsizing efforts that will ultimately impact their well-being.
3. Provide feedback to employees on their duties and job performance.
4. Provide technology to enhance job performance and improve the quality of services provided by Cooperative Extension.
5. Reevaluate job descriptions for staff employees and write them to reflect new responsibilities if needed.
6. Provide staff development which emphasize elements of specific content areas (agriculture, family and consumer studies, youth development, and management training).
7. Provide leadership training to program and division managers that will assist them in managing decline.

RECOMMENDATION FOR FURTHER STUDY

Recommendation for further studies are based on the results of this study.

1. Additional research should be conducted in other geographic areas of Extension Services undergoing downsizing that includes all divisions.
2. Research should be conducted to determine if there is a difference in perception between gender in Cooperative Extension Services and whether or not the difference reflects how programs are affected.

Cameron, K. S. (1994). Strategies for successful organizational downsizing. *Human Resource Management, 33*(2), 189–211.

Maynard, R. (1996). Boosting morale in troubled times. *Nation's Business*, 84(2), 25–30.

Nelton, S. (1996). Emotions in the workplace. *Nation's Business,* 84(2), 25–30.

Winston James, T. A. & Li-Ping Tang, T. (1996). Downsizing and the impact on survivors-A matter of justice. *Employment Relations Today*, 23(2), 33–41.

APPENDICES

Permission Letter from Personnel Departments California and Illinois

Foundations and Adult Education
College of Education
363 Bluemont Hall
1100 Mid-Campus Drive
Manhattan, KS 66506 -5305
785-532-5535

October 27, 1997

Margaret Leong
Senior Personnel Analyst
DANR, Kaiser Bldg, 6th Fl.
300 Lakeside Drive
Oakland, CA 94612-3560

Dear Ms. Leong:

This communication comes to ask your participation in a research study undertaken to learn some of the issues associated with downsizing in the American workforce. I am currently working on a doctoral study on the "Impact of Downsizing on Employee Morale and Productivity: Implications for Training" with Dr. James B. Boyer as Major Advisor.

Information obtained from the study will be anonymous and will be kept completely confidential. It is hoped that data obtained from this will be used to draw inferences and implications for enhanced leadership training. Your participation is voluntary but we would like your input on the reality of employee downsizing at this time. We would like to ask for a directory (with business addresses) of all Extension employees in your state and possibly an organizational chart. We would send the Manson Workplace Environment Analysis Inventory to them requesting their participation. (A copy of the Inventory is enclosed). We would share a copy of our findings with your office. A stamped return envelope will be provided for the return of the consent form and Inventory. No financial compensation will be provided to participants. We would appreciate your help in this effort and we applaud the work of Cooperative Extension as it positively impacts of the quality of life for all humanity. Thank you very much.

If there are any questions, please do not hesitate to contact me (B. Manson, 400 Jardine Terrace, R-12, Manhattan, Kansas 66502-- Phone: 785-565-0319) or Dr. James Boyer, Bluemont Hall, KSU, Manhattan, Kansas 66506-Phone 785-532-5554.

Bonita Manson
Researcher

James B. Boyer, Ph.D
Major Advisor

Per phone conversation, October 27, 1997 with Margaret Leong, Senior Personnel Analyst, I was advised to go online for the University of California Cooperative Extension directory search.

DANR.UCOP.edu\

UNIVERSITY OF CALIFORNIA **ATTACHMENT MEMO** GEN 100 ,8-72) Series 249–E0100	Date 11/11/97
To Bonita Manson	From Margaret Leong
Subject Org Chart	

For	Approval Signature	Initial	Comments	Discussion	Information
Please	File	Return	Draft	Take Action	Route to:

Message   As requested.

CURRENT DANR ORGANIZATIONAL STRUCTURE

UNIVERSITY OF CALIFORNIA
OFFICE OF THE VICE PRESIDENT, AGRICULTURE AND NATURAL RESOURCES

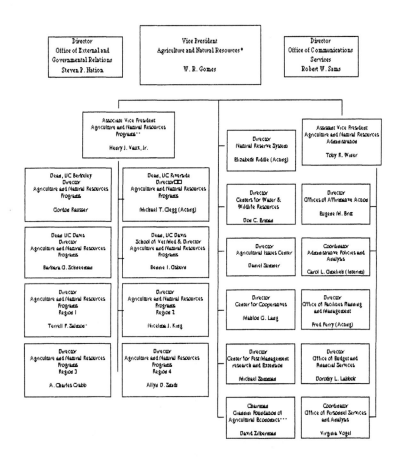

October 27, 1997

Foundations and Adult Education
College of Education
363 Bluemont Hall
1100 Mid-Campus Drive
Manhattan, KS 66506 -5305
785-532-5535

William T. McNamara
Personnel Director
Moumford Hall Room 115
1301 West Gregory Drive
Urbana, IL 61801

Dear Mr. McNamara:

This communication comes to ask your participation in a research study undertaken to learn some of the issues associated with downsizing in the American workforce. I am currently working on a doctoral study on the "Impact of Downsizing on Employee Morale and Productivity: Implications for Training" with Dr. James B. Boyer as Major Advisor.

Information obtained from the study will be anonymous and will be kept completely confidential. It is hoped that data obtained from this will be used to draw inferences and implications for enhanced leadership training. Your participation is voluntary but we would like your input on the reality of employee downsizing at this time. We would like to ask for a directory (with business addresses) of all Extension employees in your state and possibly an organizational chart. We would send the Manson Workplace Environment Analysis Inventory to them requesting their participation. (A copy of the Inventory is enclosed). We would share a copy of our findings with your office. A stamped return envelope will be provided for the return of the consent form and Inventory. No financial compensation will be provided to participants. We would appreciate your help in this effort and we applaud the work of Cooperative Extension as is positively impacts of the quality of life for all humanity. Thank you very much.

If there are any questions, please do not hesitate to contact me (B. Manson, 400 Jardine Terrace, R-12, Manhattan, Kansas 66502-- Phone: 785-565-0319) or Dr. James Boyer, Bluemont Hall, KSU, Manhattan, Kansas 66506-Phone 785-532-5554.

Bonita Manson
Researcher

James B. Boyer,Ph.D.
Major Advisor

Helping You Put Knowledge to Work

**Cooperative
Extension
Service**

College of Agricultural, Consumer,
and Environmental Sciences
University of Illinois
at Urbana-Champaign
Urbana, Illinois 61801

Dear Friend:

It's a pleasure to send you the enclosed
educational information. If the material
does not answer all your question,
please get in touch with us again.

As you may know, the Cooperative
Extension Service has one primary
purpose–to provide for you and your
neighbors the latest information on
agriculture, home economics, community resource development and related
subjects.

Through the Cooperative Extension
Service, the University of Illinois is
represented in each county by a staff of
professionally trained people.

The address of each Unit Office and
Extension Center is listed on the opposite side. We invite you to make the
Unit Office your headquarters for educational information.

Sincerely yours,

William T. McNamara
Assistant to the Director
Personnel & Staff Development

State • County • Local Groups USDA Cooperating
Illinois Natural History Survey • College of Veterinary Medicine
College of Applied Life Studies

**The Illinois Cooperative Extension Service provides
equal opportunities in programs and employment.**

COOPERATIVE EXTENSION SERVICE UNIT AND CENTER OFFICES

The Illinois Cooperative Extension Service provides equal opportunities in programs and employment

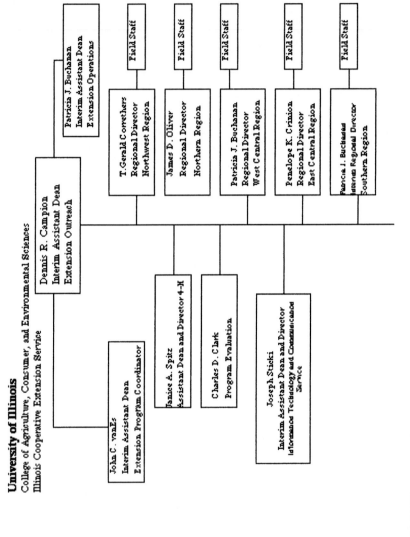

University of Illinois
College of Agriculture, Consumer, and Environmental Sciences
Illinois Cooperative Extension Service

Manson's Workplace Environment Analysis Inventory (employee's perceptions)

MANSON'S WORKPLACE ENVIRONMENT ANALYSIS INVENTORY

A tool designed to collect data on employee's
perception of job performance and employee
morale: implications for leadership training

Bonita Y. Manson
Doctoral Candidate, Curriculum & Instruction
College of Education, Kansas State University
Manhattan, Kansas 66506

This questionnaire is designed to collect data about your perceptions on employee morale and productivity: implications for leadership training.

Your participation in this study is voluntary. Your response to this questionnaire will be **anonymous** and will be kept completely **confidential**. Only summary data averaged over groups of participants will be used in the analysis.

Directions: Your responses to these statements will be used by the researcher to draw inferences and implications for leadership training programs in Cooperative Extension. Thank you for taking the time to complete this questionnaire. Please <u>do not</u> write your name on this form.

Part I: Circle the response which best represents your opinion. Some statements may require more than one response.

1. An ideal work environment should include the following:

   a. flexible   b. input on   c. personal
      scheduling   assignments   computer

   d. friendly   e. other, please list_____
      co-workers

2. An ideal method for communicating anticipated downsizing to employees is:

   a. office memos   b. employee   c. rumors
                         meetings

   d. the media   e. other, please list_____

3. The following number of employees working in county offices have been promoted in the last 5 years.

   a. 1–3   b. 3–6   c. 6–9

   d. 10 or more   e. unknown

4. The following number of employees working in county offices have been promoted in the last 10 years.

    a. 1–3   b. 3–6   c. 6–9

    d. 10 or more   e. unknown

5. My general response to an unfavorable performance evaluation is to:

    a. work harder   b. ask for assistance c. do nothing

    d. sabotage the   e. other, please list_____
       company in
       some way

6. My general response to a positive performance evaluation is to:

    a. work harder   b. work satisfactorily c. slack off

    d. expect   e. other, please list_____
       advancement

7. I first heard about Cooperative Extension's plans to downsize by:

    a. office memos   b. employee   c. rumors
                      meetings

    d. the media   e. other, please list_____

8. Rank the following employee incentives with 5 being extremely important and 1 being least important.

    ___ merit increase   ___ promotion   ___ bonus
                          opportunities

    ___ empowerment   ___ other, please list_____

Part II: Circle the answer that correctly identifies your opinion, using the following code:

        SA = Strongly agree
         A = Agree
         N = Neutral (no knowledge)
         D = Disagree
       SD = Strongly disagree

SA A N D SD   9. Employees are able to advance within the Cooperative Extension System.

SA A N D SD   10. Management is consistent in their treatment of employees.

SA A N D SD   11. Released time is allowed for staff to attend professional/skill development workshops.

SA A N D SD   12. I received a clearly written job description when I was employed by Cooperative Extension.

SA A N D SD   13. The program budget allows for employees to attend training workshops.

SA A N D SD   14. Employees are given a verbal warning about unsatisfactory performance before receiving an unfavorable job evaluation.

SA A N D SD   15. Management provides training to assist employees in performing their job.

SA A N D SD   16. Employee incentives encourages increased output.

SA A N D SD   17. Employees are able to perform at the same level as they did before Cooperative Extension downsized their county offices.

SA A N D SD   18. The employees' performance level decreased after Cooperative Extension downsized their county offices.

SA A N D SD   19. Support or assistance to perform my duties decreased after Cooperative Extension's county offices downsized.

SA A N D SD   20. The technology provided by Cooperative Extension improved my job performance.

SA A N D SD   21. Management provided timely and accurate information about their downsizing.

SA A N D SD   22. I am responsible only for duties listed on my written job description.

SA A N D SD   23. Trust can be rebuilt in organizations faced with downsizing.

SA A N D SD   24. Employees were informed of anticipated changes in Cooperative Extension by management before downsizing.

SA A N D SD   25. Management is fair in their treatment of employees.

SA A N D SD   26. My contributions to Cooperative Extension are appreciated by management.

How has management helped you to reach your performance objectives in face of downsizing?

Please share any additional **comments** you might have.

Manson's Workplace Environment Analysis Inventory (management's perceptions)

MANSON'S WORKPLACE ENVIRONMENT ANALYSIS INVENTORY

A tool designed to collect data on management's
perception of job performance and employee
morale: implications for leadership training

Bonita Y. Manson
Doctoral Candidate, Curriculum & Instruction
College of Education, Kansas State University
Manhattan, Kansas 66506

This questionnaire is designed to collect data about your perceptions on employee morale and productivity: implications for leadership training.

Your participation in this study is voluntary. Your response to this questionnaire will be **anonymous** and will be kept completely **confidential**. Only summary data averaged over groups of participants will be used in the analysis.

Directions: Your responses to these statements will be used by the researcher to draw inferences and implications for leadership training programs in Cooperative Extension. Thank you for taking the time to complete this questionnaire. Please <u>do not</u> write your name on this form.

Part I: Circle the response which best represents your opinion. Some statements may require more than one response.

1. An ideal work environment should include the following:

   a. flexible
      scheduling
   b. input on
      assignments
   c. office space

   d. friendly
      co-workers
   e. other, please list_____

2. An ideal method for communicating anticipated downsizing to employees is:

   a. office memo
   b. employee
      meeting
   c. rumors

   d. media
   e. other, please list_____

3. The following number of employees working in county offices have been promoted in the last 5 years.

   a. 1–3
   b. 3–6
   c. 6–9

   d. 10 or more
   e. other, please list_____

4. The following number of employees working in county offices have been promoted in the last 10 years.

   a. 1–3   b. 3–6   c. 6–9

   d. 10 or more   e. other, please list _____

5. Employees general response to an unfavorable performance evaluation is to:

   a. work harder   b. ask for assistance c. do nothing

   d. sabotage the   e. other, please list_____
      company in
      some way

6. Employees general response to a positive performance evaluation is to:

   a. work harder   b. work satisfactorily c. slack off

   d. expect   e. other, please list_____
      advancement

7. Employees were first notified about Cooperative Extension's plans to downsize by:

   a. office memos   b. employee   c. rumors
                        meetings

   d. the media   e. other, please list_____

8. Rank the following incentives in order of importance to employees with 5 being extremely important and 1 being least important.

   ___merit increase   ___promotion   ___bonus
                           opportunities

   ___empowerment   ___other, please list _____

Part II: Circle the answer that correctly identifies your opinion, using the following code:
SA = Strongly agree
A = Agree
N = Neutral (no knowledge)
D = Disagree
SD = Strongly disagree

SA A N D SD   9. Employees are able to advance within the Cooperative Extension System.

SA A N D SD   10. All employees are treated consistently by management.

SA A N D SD   11. Employees are allowed released time to attend professional/skill development workshops.

SA A N D SD   12. All employees are given a clearly written job description upon employment by Cooperative Extension.

SA A N D SD   13. The program budget allows for employees to attend training workshops.

SA A N D SD   14. All employees are given a verbal warning about unsatisfactory performance before receiving an unfavorable job evaluation.

SA A N D SD   15. Training is provided by management to assist employees in performing their job.

SA A N D SD   16. Employee incentives encourages increased output.

SA A N D SD   17. Employees are able to perform at the same level as they did before Cooperative Extension downsized their county offices.

SA A N D SD   18. The employees' performance level decreased after Cooperative Extension downsized their county offices.

SA A N D SD   19. Support or assistance provided by management decreased after Cooperative Extension county offices.

SA A N D SD   20. The technology provided by Cooperative Extension has improved employees' job performance.

SA A N D SD   21. Management provided timely and accurate information about their downsizing.

SA A N D SD   22. Employees are responsible only for duties listed on my written job description.

SA A N D SD   23. Trust can be rebuilt in organizations faced with downsizing.

SA A N D SD   24. Employees were informed of anticipated changes in Cooperative Extension by management before downsizing.

SA A N D SD   25. Management is fair in their treatment of employees.

SA A N D SD   26. The employees' contributions to Cooperative Extension are appreciated by management.

What are you doing to maintain the mission of Cooperative Extension after staff reduction?

Please share any additional **comments** you would like to add.

Informed Consent Document

Kansas State University

Office of Research and
Sponsored Programs
103 Fairchild Hall
Manhattan, KS 66506 - 1103
785 532-6195
Fax 785-532-5944

TO: James B. Boyer   Proposal Number: 1416
         Education
         Bluemont Hall

FROM: Clive Fullagar, Chair
         Committee on Research Involving Human Subjects

DATE: October 10, 1997

RE: Proposal #1416, entitled "The Impact of Downsizing on Employee Morale and
         Productivity: Implications for Training."

The Committee on Research Involving Human Subjects has reviewed and approved the proposal
identified above. In giving its approval, the Committee has determined that:

☒   There is no more than minimal risk to the subjects.
☐   There is greater than minimal risk to the subjects.

This approval applies only to the proposal currently on file and is effective for one year from the
date of this memo. Any change affecting human subjects must be approved by the Committee prior
to implementation. All approved proposals are subject to review, which may include the
examination of records connected with the projects. Unanticipated problems involving risk to
subjects or to others must be reported immediately to the Chair of the Committee on research
Involving Human Subjects and, if the subjects are KSU students, to the Director of the Student
Health Center.

Prior to involving human subjects, properly executed informed consent must be obtained from each
subject or from an authorized representative. Each subject must be furnished with a copy of the
informed consent document for his or her personal records, and documentation must be kept on file
for at least three years after the project ends. The identification of particular human subjects in any
publication is an invasion of privacy and requires a separately executed informed consent. A copy
of your informed consent documentation as approved by the Committee is enclosed.

INFORMED CONSENT

You are invited to participate in a study on employee morale and productivity: implication for leadership training. I hope to discover how job performance is impacted by employee morale and trust in order to draw inferences and implications for leadership training programs. A Workplace Analysis Inventory will be administered to all participants.

If you have any questions, now or in the future, please ask them. Please contact, Bonita Manson, at 400 Jardine Terrace R-12, Manhattan, Kansas, 785-565-0319, or Dr. James Boyer, Major Advisor, 785-532-5554, Bluemont Hall, Kansas State University, Manhattan, Kansas. All data will be reported as grouped data and confidentiality of your replies is guaranteed by the researchers. If you decide to take part, you may withdraw your consent of participation at any time.

Are you willing to be interviewed? _____ Yes _____ No

If I am selected to be interviewed, the researcher has my permission to tape record this session: _____ yes _____ no
I understand that typed transcripts of these taped interviews will be made and that both the tapes and typed copies will be kept confidential and anonymous.

I have read the above statements and have been fully advised of the procedures to be used in this study. I volunteer to participate.

_____   _____
Signature   Date

Demographic Data

MANSON'S WORKPLACE
ENVIRONMENT ANALYSIS INVENTORY

Personal Data

Gender: ___ male   ___ female

Age: _____ less than 21   _____ 21–30   _____ 31–40
         _____ 41–50   _____ 50 or more

Educational background: ___ high school diploma
                         ___ 1 year college/technical school
                         ___ 2 years college/technical school
                         ___ 3 years college
                         ___ 4 years college
                         ___ Master's degree
                         ___ Master's degree plus additional hours
                         ___ Doctoral or terminal degree

Years experience with your
   employer: ___ less than 1 year   ___ 1–5 years
                      ___ 6–10 years   ___ 11–15 years
                      ___ 16 or more

Job Title: _____

Rights of Human Subjects Checklist

APPLICATION FOR REVIEW
INSTITUTIONAL REVIEW BOARD
FOR RESEARCH INVOLVING HUMAN SUBJECTS

Please answer all questions. *Applications judged by the chair of the IRB to be illegible, incomplete, or vague will be returned to the Principal Investigator for revision. Attach continuation sheets as necessary. Submit three copies (the original and two photocopies) to the Institutional Review Board, 103 Fairchild Hall.*

I.   **Identification:**
    Principal Investigator (*Must be a Faculty Member*): Dr. James B. Boyer
    Department or Division: Education   Campus Phone: 532-5554   E-mail Address: _____
    Descriptive Title of the Proposed Research Project: The Impact of Downsizing on Employee
     Morale and Productivity: Implications for Training

    Names of Students or Staff Associated with the Project: Bonita Manson, Dr. James Boyer,
     Dr. Stephen Bollman, Dr. Mary Evan Griffith, & Dr. John H ortin
    Funding Agency or Source (if applicable): _____

II. **Type of IRB Application:**
    ☒ New (Complete the remainder of the application and submit it to the IRB.)
    ☐ Previously approved. IRB No: _____ (Check the appropriate category below.)
        ☐ Changes Only in Title and/or Funding Agency (Skip to Section VIII of the application.)
        ☐ Modification/Addendum (Complete the remainder of the application. Explain the planned changes.)
        ☐ Triennial Review (Complete the remainder of the application.)

III. **Project Information:** (If the response to any of the following is "yes," explain on continuation pages.)

Yes	No	Does the research involve any of the following?
☐	☒	a. Deception of subjects
☐	☒	b. Shock or other forms of punishment
☐	☒	c. Sexually explicit materials or questions
☐	☒	d. Handling of money or other valuable commodities
☐	☒	e. Extraction of blood or other bodily fluids
☐	☒	f. Questions about drug use
☐	☒	g. Questions about sexual orientation, sexual experience, or sexual abuse
☐	☒	h. Purposeful creation of anxiety
☐	☒	i. Any procedure that might be viewed as invasion of privacy
☐	☒	j. Physical exercise or stress
☐	☒	k. Administration of substances (food, drugs, etc.) to subjects
☐	☒	l. Any procedure that might place subjects at risk. Specify _____

IV. **Subject Information:** (If the response to any of the following is "yes," explain on continuation pages.)

Yes	No	Does the research involve subjects from any of the following categories?
☐	☒	a. Under 18 years of age
☐	☒	b. Over 65 years of age
☒	☐	c. Physically or mentally disabled
☐	☒	d. Economically or educationally disadvantaged
☐	☒	e. Unable to provide their own legal informed consent
☐	☒	f. Pregnant females as target population
☐	☒	g. Victims
☐	☒	h. Subjects in institutions (e.g., prisons, nursing homes, halfway houses)

IRB Application Form (January 31, 1995)

V. Researcher Information:

Yes	No	Answer the following questions about the researchers.
☒	☐	a. Are all researchers aware of the University guidelines regarding rights of human subjects? (If the answer is "no," explain on continuation pages.)
☒	☐	b. Are all researchers aware of plans for responding to any emergencies or other problems arising from the research (such as dealing with upset or emotionally distraught subjects)?
☒	☐	c. Is the research part of a thesis or dissertation? If "yes," then indicate which.

    ☐ Thesis   ☒ Dissertation

Name of Graduate Student: __Bonita Manson__

List the members of the committee: __Dr. James Boyer, Dr. Stephen Bollman, Dr. Mary Evan Griffith, & Dr. John Hortin__

VI. Risks and Benefits: (Note: the IRB retains final authority for determining risk status of a project)

Yes	No	Answer the following questions about the research.
☐	☒	a. In your opinion, does the research involve more than minimal risk to subjects? ("Minimal risk" means that "the risks of harm anticipated in the proposed research are not greater, considering probability and magnitude, than those ordinarily encountered in daily life or during the performance of routine physical or psychological examinations or tests.") If the answer is "yes," explain on continuation pages and attach an explanation of the benefits of the research to the subjects and to the discipline or profession.)
☐	☒	b. Are any emergencies or adverse reactions (physical, psychological, social, legal, or emotional) probable as a result of the research? (If "yes," then explain how they will be handled.)
☐	☒	c. Do subjects leave the study or experiment in approximately the same emotional state as they began? (If "no," then explain how distress will be handled. In most cases, this means informing subjects that if they become upset, want to talk about the study or related experiences, and so on, you are available. You should provide subjects with your office number and telephone number.)

VII. Informed Consent:

Yes	No	Answer the following questions about the informed consent procedures.
☒	☐	a. Are you using a written informed consent form? (If "yes," include a copy. If "no," explain why and describe how consent will be obtained.)
☒	☐	b. Do you preserve the anonymity of subjects? (If "no," explain why and describe how you will protect the identity of subjects.)
☒	☐	c. Are subjects debriefed about the purposes, consequences, and benefits of the research? (If "no," explain why.)

VIII. Assurance by Principal Investigator:

I agree to conduct this research project in accordance with *Federal Policy for the Protection of Human Subjects*, effective August 19, 1991, and with the Kansas State University "Assurance of Compliance with HHS Regulations for Protection of Human Research Subjects." No changes in my research protocol will be implemented without the prior review and approval of the Institutional Review Board.

Signed _James B. Boyer_   Date _10-2-1997_

FOR OFFICE USE ONLY

I have examined this Application for review of Research Involving Human Subjects and make the following determination:

___ This project is exempt from further review by the IRB.

___ This project is eligible for expedited review.

   ___ I recommend unconditional approval. ___ I recommend conditional approval (append conditions).

___ This project should receive complete IRB committee review.

Signed _____   Date _____

Legal Requirements and Definitions for Research Involving Human Subjects

The legal authority for the Internal Review Board (IRB) comes from the Federal Policy for the Protection of Human Subjects (described in 45 CFR Part 46). In addition, Kansas State University has on file with the Public Health Service a statement of assurance committing the University to compliance with Federal Policy. No research involving humans may be undertaken without prior review and approval by the IRB.

These following definitions are taken from the Federal Policy for Protection of Human Subjects (45 CFR Part 46).

"*Research* means a systematic investigation, including research development, testing, and evaluation, designed to develop or contribute to generalizable knowledge."

"*Human subject* means a living individual about whom an investigator (whether professional or student) conducting research obtains
(1) data through intervention or interaction with the individual, or
(2) identifiable private information."

"*Intervention* includes both physical procedures by which data are gathered and manipulations of the subject or the subject's environment that are performed for research purposes."

"*Interactions* includes communication or interpersonal contact between investigator and subject."

"*Private information* includes information about behavior that occurs in a context in which an individual can reasonably expect that no observation or recording is taking place, ... and which the individual can reasonably expect will not be made public."

"*IRB approval* means the determination of the IRB that the research has been reviewed and may be conducted at an institution within the constraints set forth by ... institutional and federal requirements....An IRB shall have the authority to suspend ... research that is not being conducted in accordance with the IRB's requirements."

"No investigator may involve a human being as a subject in research unless the investigator has obtained the legally effective *informed consent* of the subject or the subject's legally authorized representative."

"An IRB shall require *documentation* of informed consent.... Informed consent will be sought from each prospective subject or the subject's legally authorized representative. Informed consent will be appropriately documented...by the use of a written form approved by the IRB."

"When some or all of the subjects are likely to be *vulnerable*..., such as children,... or economically or educationally disadvantaged persons, additional safeguards (should) be included...to protect the rights and welfare of these subjects."

Steps in the Process of Review by the IRB

1. A completed Application for Review (the original and two photocopies) should be submitted to the Chair of the Institutional Review Board (IRB), c/o the Committee Secretary, 103 Fairchild Hall. (When necessary, a letter to a prospective funding agency will be issued stating that the proposed research protocol is under review and that the IRB will make a decision within 60 days.)

2. The Chair assigns the application to two reviewers. The reviewers may either make a recommendation or call for complete committee review.

3. If the reviewers decide that the research project is *exempt* and the Chair concurs, the Principal Investigator will be informed in writing, and the project will be assigned an IRB number. If there are stipulations, they will be specified in a letter to the Principal Investigator and must be addressed before the project can be approved and assigned an IRB number.

4. If the reviewers decide that the project is eligible for *expedited review* and the Chair concurs, then approval can be granted either with or without stipulations. If there are stipulations, they will be specified in a letter to the Principal Investigator and must be addressed before the project can be approved and assigned an IRB number.

5. If the reviewers or the Chair decides that the project should receive *complete committee review*, the Chair places the application on the agenda of the next regular meeting of the IRB or convenes a special meeting. The committee may approve the application as submitted, approve it with stipulations, or disapprove it. The action of the committee will be reported in writing to the investigator. Any stipulations must be addressed before the project can be approved and assigned an IRB number.

6. Either the committee or the investigator can request that the investigator be present at the part of the meeting of the IRB when a specific project is being considered.

7. If required, a letter describing the decision of the IRB will be addressed to the funding agency. Normally, this letter will be forwarded to the agency by the investigator.

IRB Application Form (January 31, 1995)

Legal Requirements and Definitions for Research Involving Human Subjects

The legal authority for the Internal Review Board (IRB) comes from the Federal Policy for the Protection of Human Subjects (described in 45 CFR Part 46). In addition, Kansas State University has on file with the Public Health Service a statement of assurance committing the University to compliance with Federal Policy. No research involving humans may be undertaken without prior review and approval by the IRB.

These following definitions are taken from the Federal Policy for Protection of Human Subjects (45 CFR Part 46).

"*Research* means a systematic investigation, including research development, testing, and evaluation, designed to develop or contribute to generalizable knowledge."

"*Human subject* means a living individual about whom an investigator (whether professional or student) conducting research obtains
(1) data through intervention or interaction with the individual, or
(2) identifiable private information."

"*Intervention* includes both physical procedures by which data are gathered and manipulations of the subject or the subject's environment that are performed for research purposes."

"*Interactions* includes communication or interpersonal contact between investigator and subject."

"*Private information* includes information about behavior that occurs in a context in which an individual can reasonably expect that no observation or recording is taking place, ... and which the individual can reasonably expect will not be made public."

"*IRB approval* means the determination of the IRB that the research has been reviewed and may be conducted at an institution within the constraints set forth by ... institutional and federal requirements....An IRB shall have the authority to suspend ... research that is not being conducted in accordance with the IRB's requirements."

"No investigator may involve a human being as a subject in research unless the investigator has obtained the legally effective *informed consent* of the subject or the subject's legally authorized representative."

"An IRB shall require *documentation* of informed consent.... Informed consent will be sought from each prospective subject or the subject's legally authorized representative. Informed consent will be appropriately documented...by the use of a written form approved by the IRB."

"When some or all of the subjects are likely to be *vulnerable*..., such as children,... or economically or educationally disadvantaged persons, additional safeguards (should) be included...to protect the rights and welfare of these subjects."

Steps in the Process of Review by the IRB

1. A completed Application for Review (the original and two photocopies) should be submitted to the Chair of the Institutional Review Board (IRB), c/o the Committee Secretary, 103 Fairchild Hall. (When necessary, a letter to a prospective funding agency will be issued stating that the proposed research protocol is under review and that the IRB will make a decision within 60 days.)

2. The Chair assigns the application to two reviewers. The reviewers may either make a recommendation or call for complete committee review.

3. If the reviewers decide that the research project is *exempt* and the Chair concurs, the Principal Investigator will be informed in writing, and the project will be assigned an IRB number. If there are stipulations, they will be specified in a letter to the Principal Investigator and must be addressed before the project can be approved and assigned an IRB number.

4. If the reviewers decide that the project is eligible for *expedited review* and the Chair concurs, then approval can be granted either with or without stipulations. If there are stipulations, they will be specified in a letter to the Principal Investigator and must be addressed before the project can be approved and assigned an IRB number.

5. If the reviewers or the Chair decides that the project should receive *complete committee review*, the Chair places the application on the agenda of the next regular meeting of the IRB or convenes a special meeting. The committee may approve the application as submitted, approve it with stipulations, or disapprove it. The action of the committee will be reported in writing to the investigator. Any stipulations must be addressed before the project can be approved and assigned an IRB number.

6. Either the committee or the investigator can request that the investigator be present at the part of the meeting of the IRB when a specific project is being considered.

7. If required, a letter describing the decision of the IRB will be addressed to the funding agency. Normally, this letter will be forwarded to the agency by the investigator.

IRB Application Form (January 31, 1995)

In response to IVc. Does the research involve subjects from any of the following categories?

    c. Physically or mentally disabled.

The Cooperative Extension System, a nationwide educational network established through legislation, is a partnership of the U. S. department of agriculture, State land-grant universities, and the county government.

They prohibit discrimination in their programs on the bias of race, color, national origin, sex, religion, age, disability, political beliefs and marital or familial status.

Accommodations are provided for persons who require alternative means of communication.

The University is an equal opportunity employer.

Follow-up Mailing

MANSON'S WORKPLACE ENVIRONMENT ANALYSIS

Three weeks ago you received a short survey on your perceptions of employee morale and productivity after downsizing. Your response is important to this study.

If you have already returned your completed survey please accept my sincere thanks for your participation.

Notify me collect at (785) 565-0319 if you need a replacement survey. Thanks, Bonita Manson, Kansas State University, School of Education.

MANSON'S WORKPLACE ENVIRONMENT ANALYSIS

If you have mailed your survey, please disregard this final call for participation. Thank you for your willingness to participate.

If you have not yet completed the survey, please reconsider and take the 7 minutes it takes to complete it. Your perceptions are important to this study. This data will be used to improve leadership training for management.

I will be completing all data collection on February 13th. Again, thank you for your participation.

Inventory Analysis Matrix

Workplace Analysis Matrix

_____I_____I_____II_____I_____III

Information 1, 2, 3, 4, 5, 6, 13

_____I_____I_____

Morale   7, 8, 9, 10, 11   1, 5, 6, 22, 23,   3, 4, 13, 21
             12, 19   24 , 25, 26

_____I_____I_____

Productivity 15, 16, 17, 18   8, 11
             19, 20

_____I_____I_____

Trust   21, 22, 23, 24   7, 9, 10   12
             25, 26

_____I_____I_____

Letter of Permission for Pilot Study

October 11, 1997

Laurie Chandler
County Director
1740 SW Western Avenue
Topeka, KS 66604-3095

Dear Ms. Chandler:

Enclosed you will find copies of my research instrument for my dissertation titled, The Impact of Downsizing on Employee Morale and Productivity: Implications for Training. This instrument will be used to find out information about job performance, employee morale, and trust. I will be concerned with issues of morale and productivity while noting factors of advanced training and seniority in Cooperative Extension employment. There will be particular attention to difference of perception between staff employees and those with managerial or supervisory responsibilities.

I would like very much if you and your staff can review this instrument to make sure it is clear and concise. Employee copies are enclosed for clerical, paraprofessional, and an extension agent. A management copy, pink in color, is included for you to complete. In addition, I also included a copy of interview questions. I would like to know how much time is needed to complete the instrument. Please respond with any comments. I would particularly like to know if any statements are unclear or redundant. I will be conducting my research with Cooperative Extension in California and Illinois.

Please return these copies in the enclosed envelope by October 27, 1997. Thank you for your assistance.

Sincerely,

Bonita Manson

October 11, 1997

Alan Ladd
County Director
110 Courthouse Plaza
Manhattan, KS 66502

Dear Mr. Ladd:

Enclosed you will find copies of my research instrument for my dissertation titled, The Impact of Downsizing on Employee Morale and Productivity: Implications for Training. This instrument will be used to find out information about job performance, employee morale, and trust. I will be concerned with issues of morale and productivity while noting factors of advanced training and seniority in Cooperative Extension employment. There will be particular attention to difference of perception between staff employees and those with managerial or supervisory responsibilities.

I would like very much if you and your staff can review this instrument to make sure it is clear and concise. Employee copies are enclosed for clerical, paraprofessional, and an extension agent. A management copy, pink in color, is included for you to complete. In addition, I also included a copy of interview questions. I would like to know how much time is needed to complete the instrument. Please respond with any comments. I would particularly like to know if any statements are unclear or redundant. I will be conducting my research with Cooperative Extension in California and Illinois.

Please return these copies in the enclosed envelope by October 27, 1997. Thank you for your assistance.

Sincerely,

Bonita Manson

Interview Questions

MANSON'S WORKPLACE
ENVIRONMENT INTERVIEW QUESTIONS

This questionnaire is designed to collect data about your perceptions on employee morale and productivity: implications for leadership training.

Your participation in this study is voluntary. Your response to this questionnaire will be **anonymous** and will be kept completely **confidential.** Only summary data averaged over groups of participants will be used in the analysis.

Directions: Your responses to these questions will be used by the researcher to draw inferences and implications for leadership training programs in Cooperative Extension. Thank you for your participation in this interview.

1. Were you aware that Cooperative Extension is/was in the process of downsizing?

_____

   a. How did this information affect you? _____

_____

_____

   b. Did this information impact your job outcomes? _____

_____

2. Do you feel secure in your job? _____ If not, why? _____

_____

_____

3. Do you believe Cooperative Extension provides upward mobility to its employees?

_____

_____

   a. Are you interested in advancing within the university system? _____

   b. Have you had an opportunity to advance within the university system?

_____

c. How does Cooperative Extension assist or prepare its employees for advancement? _____

_____

_____

4. If upward mobility is possible, do you think downsizing will impact your chances for advancement? _____

_____

5. How has Cooperative Extension helped you to reach your performance objectives since downsizing? _____

_____

_____

6. In what way can Cooperative Extension assist you in reaching your performance objectives? _____

_____

_____

Bibliography

Adams, J. S. (1965). Inequity in social exchange. In L. Berkowitz (Ed.), *Advances in Experimental Social Psychology* (pp. 267–299). New York: Academic Press.

Adams, J. S., & Rosenbaum, W. B. (1962). The relationship of worker productivity to cognitive dissonance about wage inequities. *Journal of Applied Psychology, 46,* 161–164.

Agria, M. (1996). Downsizing can lead to drop in employee morale. (Online). World Wide Web. thonline.com/news.

Akin, G. & Hopelain, D. (1986). Finding the culture of productivity. *Organizational Dynamics, 14(3),* 19–32.

Armstrong-Strassen, M. & Latack, J. C. (1992). Coping with work-force reduction: The effects of layoff exposure on survivors' reactions. *Proceedings of the Annual Meeting of the Academy of Management,* 207–211.

Behn, R. D. (1978). Closing a government facility. *Public Administration Reviews, 38 (4),* 332–338.

Benson, M. A. (1995). Behind the smoke and mirrors of reorganization: An esemplastic taxonomy for understanding individual psychosocial response to survivorship (stress). *Dissertation Abstracts International, 55(7),* 2034A.

Berenbeim, R. E. (1986). *Company programs to ease the impact of shutdowns,* New York, NY: The Conference Board, Inc.

Best, J. W. & Kahn, J. V. (1998). *Research in Education* (8th ed.). Boston: Allyn & Bacon.

Bitz, G. P. (1997). Downsizing at the defense finance and accounting service (DFAS). *The Government Accountants Journal, 45(4),* 14, 20–22.

Blank, M. D. (1996). The implications on organizational learning as the result of downsizing. *Dissertation Abstracts International, 57(6),* 2334A.

Blonder, M. D. (1976). Organization repercussions of personnel cutbacks: Effects of layoffs on retained employees. Unpublished doctoral dissertation. City University of New York.

Bogdan, R. C. & Biklen, S. K. (1998). *Qualitative Research in Education* (3rd ed.). Boston: Allyn & Bacon.

Bollar, S. L. (1996). The impact of organizational culture on employee work attitudes, readiness for chance, and organizational performance. *Dissertation Abstracts International, 57(3),* 2195B.

Borg, W. R. & Gall, M. D. (1989). *Educational Research An Introduction* (5th ed.). New York: Longman.

Borucki, C., & Barnett, C. (1990). Restructuring for self-renewal: Navistar international corporation. *Academy of Management Executive, 4(1),* 36–49.

Bradley, J. (1993). Methodological issues and practices in qualitative research. *Library Quarterly, 63* (4), 431–449.

Brockner, J. (1988). The effects of work layoffs on survivors. Research, theory, and practice. *Research in Organizational Behavior, 10,* 213–255.

Brockner, J., Davy, J. & Carter, C. (1985). Layoffs, self-esteem, and survivor guilt: Motivational affective, and attitudinal consequences. *Organizational Behavior and Human Decision Processes, 36(2),* 229–244.

Brockner, J., Glover, S. & Blonder, M. D. (1988). (Predictors of survivors' job involvement following layoffs: A field study. *Journal of Applied Psychology, 73(3),* 436–442.

Brockner, J., Glover, S., Reed, T., DeWitt, R. & O'Malley, M. (1987). Survivors' reactions to layoffs: We get by with a little help for our fiends. *Administrative Science Quarterly, 32(4),* 526–541.

Buchanan, C. E. (1996). Organizational downsizing: Effects on human resource development in organizations in St. Louis metropolitan area (Missouri). *Dissertation Abstracts International, 57(6),* 2334. (University Microfilm No. AAC 9634973).

Burack, E. H. & Singh, R. S. (1995). The new employment relations compact. The *Journal of The Human Resource Planning Society, 18* (1), 12–19.

Cameron, K. S., Sutton, R. I., and Whetten, D. A. (1988). Issues in organizational decline. In K. S. Cameron, R. I. Sutton, and D. A. Whetten (Eds.) *Readings in Organizational Decline,* (pp. 3–19).

Cascio, W. F. (1993). Downsizing: What do we know? What have we learned? *Academy of Management Executive, 7* (1), 95–104.

Caudron, S. (1996). Teach downsizing survivors how to thrive. *Personnel Journal, 75* (1), 38–48.

Caudron, S. (1996). Keeping spirits up when times are down. *Personnel Journal, 75* (8), 26–31.

Caudron, S. (1996). Rebuilding employee trust. *Training & Development, 50* (8), 18–21.

Charles, C. M. (1995). Educational research and its sources of data. *Introduction to Educational Research* (2nd ed.). New York: Longman.

Curtis, R. L. (1989). Cutbacks, management, and human relations: Meanings for organizational theory and research. *Human Relations, 42(8)*, 671–689.

Day, S. (1996). The impact of communication on employee reaction to organizational change: A case study. *Masters Abstracts International, 34(2)*, 469.

Demers, R., Forrer, S. E., Leibowitz, Z., & Cahill, C. (1996). Commitment to change. *Training & Development, 35* (2), 203–216.

Dillman, D. A. (1978). (Ed.). *Mail and Telephone Surveys.* New York: John Wiley & Sons.

Dixon, N. M. (1996). The implications on organizational learning as the result of downsizing. *Dissertation Abstracts International, 56*(10), 3823. (University Microfilm No. AAC 9604262).

Dodaro, G. L. (1997). Lessons learned in reshaping GAO. *The Government Accountants Journal, 45(4)*, 15, 32–33.

Duron, S. A. (1993). The reality of downsizing: What are the productivity outcomes? *Dissertation Abstracts International, 54(9)*, 4953B.

Ewing, J. B. (1994). The impact of total quality improvement program on the perceptions and feelings of middle managers and hourly employees. *Dissertation Abstracts International, 55(6)*, 1455, (University Microfilm No. AAC 1429727).

Feldman, D. C. (1996). Managing careers in downsizing firms. *Human Resource Management, 35* (2), 145–161.

Freeman, S. J. (1994). Organizational downsizing as convergence or reorientation: Implications for human resource management. *Human Resource Management, 33(2)*, 213–238.

Galpin, T. (1995). Pruning the grapevine. *Training & Development, 49* (4), 28–33.

Gambill, T. R. (1979). Career counseling: Too little, too late? *Training & Development Journal, 33* (2), 24–27.

Gephart, M. A. (1995). The road to high performance. *Training & Development, 49* (6), 29–38.

Gill, S. J. (1995). Shifting gears for high performance. *Training & Development, 49* (5), 25–31.

Greenhalgh, L. (1982). Maintaining organizational effectiveness during organizational retrenchment. *Journal of Applied Behavioral Science, 18*, 155–170.

Henkoff, R. (1990). Cost cutting: How to do it right. *Fortune, 121* (8), 40–49.

Jick, T. D. (1979). Mixing qualitative and quantitative methods: Triangulation in action. *Administrative Science Quarterly, 24* (4), 602–611.

Koesterer, S. J. (1995). The relationship between demographic variables and job insecurity of the survivors of a corporate downsizing. *Dissertation Abstracts International, 55(12),* 3915A.

Kovach, K. A. (1995). Employee motivation: Addressing a crucial factor in you organization's performance. *Employment Relations Today, 22* (3), 93–107.

Kuh, G. D. & Andreas, R. E. (1991) It's about time: Using qualitative methods in student life studies. *Journal of College Student Development, 32* (3), 397–405.

Kuttner, R. (1993). Talking marriage and thinking one-night stand. *Business Week,* October 18.

Lee, C. (1997). Trust me. *Training, 34* (1), 28–37.

Leedy, P. D. (1993). Research methodology: Qualitative or quantitative? Practical *Research Planning and Design* (5th ed., pp. 137–147). New York: MacMillan.

Lehrer, S. (1997). Effectively coping with downsizing: A four-phase model. *The Government Accountants Journal, 45(4),* 16–19.

Levine, C. H. (1978). Organizational decline and cutback management. *Public Administration Review, 38,* 316–325.

Levine, C. H. (1979). More on cutback management: Hard questions for hard times. *Public Administration Review, 39,* 179–183.

Lim, V. K. (1996). Job insecurity and its outcomes: Moderating effects of work-based and nonwork-based social support. *Human Relations, 49* (2), 171–194. *Personnel Management, 24* (4), 475–492.

Lincoln, Y. S. & Guba, E. G. (1985). *Naturalistic Inquiry.* Newbury Park, CA: Sage.

Maynard, R. (1996). Boosting morale in troubled times. *Nation's Business, 84* (2), 25–30.

Middlebrook, J. F. (1996). How to manage individual performance. *Training & Development, 50 (9),* 45–48.

Morris, T. (1996, December–January). Employee satisfaction maximizing the return on human capital. *CMA Magazine,* 15.

Neal, A. (1994). Surviving downsizing: An orgnizational case study. *Dissertation Abstracts International, 54(8),* 4430A.

Nelton, S. (1996). Emotions in the workplace. *Nation's Business, 84* (2). 25–30.

Pfeffer, J. (1995). Producing sustainable competitive advantage through the effective management of people. *Academy of Management Executive, 9* (1), 55–69.

Puffer, S. M. (1987). Prosocial behavior, noncomplaint behavior, and work performance among commission salespeople. *Journal of Applied Psychology, 72,* 615–621.

Reece, B. (1996). The impact of communication on employee reaction to organizational change: A case study. *Masters Abstracts International, 34* (2), 469. (University Microfilm No. AAC 1376288).

Richardson, P. & Denton D. K. (1996). Communicating change. *Human Resource Management, 35* (2), 203–216.

Roach, S. S. (1996). The hollow ring of the productivity revival. *Harvard Business Review, 74* (6), 81–89.

Rowley, W., Crist, T., & Presley, I. (1995). Partnerships for productivity. *Training & Development, 49 (1),* 53–55.

Rubach, L. (1995). Downsizing: How quality is affected as companies shrink. *Quality Progress, 28* (4), 23–25.

Schweiger, D. M. & Denisi, A. S. (1991). Communication with employers following a merger: A longitudinal field experiment. *Academy of Management Journal, 34(1),* 110–135.

Shannon, D. (1996). The impact of communication on employee reaction to organizational change: A case study. *Masters Abstracts International, 34* (2), AAC 1376288.

Strebel P. (1996). Why do employees resist change? *Harvard Business Review, 74* (3), 86–92.

Sugalski, T. D., Manzo, L. S., & Meadows, J. L. (1995). Resource link: Reestablishing the employment relationship in an era of downsizing. *Human Resource Management, 34* (3), 389–403.

Ting, Y. (1996). Workforce reductions and terminations benefits in governments: The case of advance notice. *Public Personnel Management, 25* (20), 183–198.

Van Maanen, J. (Ed.). Reclaiming qualitative methods for organizational research: A preface. *Administrative Science Quarterly, 24* (4), 520–526.

Whetten, D. A. (1980). Sources, responses, and effects of organizational decline. In J. R. Kimberly, R. H. Miles and Associates (Eds.), *The Organizational Life Cycle,* (pp. 342–374). San Francisco, CA: Josey-Boss Publishers.

Winston James, T. A. & Li-Ping Tang, T. (1996). Downsizing and the impact on survivors - A matter of justice. *Employment Relations Today, 23* (2), 33–41.

Zammuto, R. F. (1982). Organizational decline and management education. *Exchange: The Organizational Behavior Teaching Journal, VII* (3), 5–12.

Author Index

Subject Index